The Long Road Ahead

The Long Road Ahead

Battling the Storms

B.J. Thomas

XULON PRESS

Xulon Press
555 Winderley Pl, Suite 225
Maitland, FL 32751
407.339.4217
www.xulonpress.com

© 2021 by B.J. Thomas

All rights reserved solely by the author. The author guarantees all contents are original and do not infringe upon the legal rights of any other person or work. No part of this book may be reproduced in any form without the permission of the author.

Due to the changing nature of the Internet, if there are any web addresses, links, or URLs included in this manuscript, these may have been altered and may no longer be accessible. The views and opinions shared in this book belong solely to the author and do not necessarily reflect those of the publisher. The publisher therefore disclaims responsibility for the views or opinions expressed within the work.

Unless otherwise indicated, Scripture quotations taken from the Holy Bible, New International Version (NIV). Copyright © 1973, 1978, 1984, 2011 by Biblica, Inc.™. Used by permission. All rights reserved.

Paperback ISBN-13: 978-1-6628-3485-1
Hardcover ISBN-13: 978-1-6628-3486-8
eBook ISBN-13: 978-1-6628-3487-5

Table of Contents

Chapter 1	....	1
Chapter 2	....	3
Chapter 3	....	6
Chapter 4	....	9
Chapter 5	....	12
Chapter 6	....	15
Chapter 7	....	18
Chapter 8	....	22
Chapter 9	....	25
Chapter 10	....	27
Chapter 11	....	36
Chapter 12	....	44
Chapter 13	....	49
Chapter 14	....	52
Chapter 15	....	57
Chapter 16	....	63
Chapter 17	....	65
Chapter 18	....	68
Chapter 19	....	72
Chapter 20	....	75
Chapter 21	....	79
Chapter 22	....	82
Chapter 23	....	86
Chapter 24	....	89

The Long Road Ahead

Chapter 25	....	93
Chapter 26	....	95
Chapter 27	....	98
Chapter 28	....	100
Chapter 29	....	102
Chapter 30	....	106
Chapter 31	....	109
Chapter 32	....	111
Chapter 33	....	113
Chapter 34	....	115
Chapter 35	....	117
Chapter 36	....	120
Chapter 37	....	123
Chapter 38	....	125
Chapter 39	....	128
Chapter 40	....	130
Chapter 41	....	132
Chapter 42	....	135
Chapter 43	....	137
Chapter 44	....	139
Chapter 45	....	142
Chapter 46	....	144
Chapter 47	....	146
Chapter 48	....	149
Chapter 49	....	154
Chapter 50	....	159

Chapter 1

Scared and afraid Elizabeth sat in her jail cell, wondering how in the world did she get there. Her life begins to flash through her mind. Is this my destiny? Is this the end of my story? Where did I go wrong? It seemed like her life was over, at least that was all she could see. The consequences of her choices, may have caused her everything. Nineteen and behind bars, was not the life Elizabeth had pictured. It started her senior year in high school, when Elizabeth fell for a tall slender brown-skinned upper classman, named Jacob. Elizabeth never thought she could be with it someone like him. It was an improbable romance. They were the complete opposites, in a love cycle, traveling down a long road with no concerns of the consequences. Elizabeth was considered to be a plain jane, a common girl who loved life. She was simple and came from a lower-class one parent family background. Jacob was not so simple; he was quite popular, starred on the basketball team

The Long Road Ahead

and had nothing more than the best. Somehow, their paths crossed and fate did the rest. They were an idol, they were good together. Elizabeth and Jacob seemed to be the perfect couple, at least that was how it appeared. Love is a wonder feeling, when it's the lack there of in one's life. She fell for him hard!

Jacob was Elizabeth first real relationship and she was all in. They were carelessly in love and she was his completely! Elizabeth enjoyed every moment of their encounters.

Chapter 2

Jacob and Elizabeth spent most of their free time together, when they were able. It was a young love and it made Elizabeth on top of the world, blinded by everything else around her. Carelessly in love, Elizabeth's magical reality came to a halt. Elizabeth became pregnant! She was scared and confused. How could this have happened? Elizabeth really knew nothing about love or the consequences of given yourself to one that's not your husband. Elizabeth could not tell her mother. She would kill her. Elizabeth was still in school and had no means of taking care of herself or a child. She turned to Jacob hoping they could figure things out together. She knew it would be hard, but she believed their love was stronger, than a little bump in the road.

What Elizabeth thought was the greatest love of all, turned into the beginning of the darkness era of her life. Jacob told his parents of the situation

The Long Road Ahead

and they asked Elizabeth over to discuss the pregnancy. Elizabeth was nervous, even still, she knew Jacob would be there for her. She went to Jacob's house to talk, only to find out that shewas then only one on trial. Jacobs parents demanded that Elizabeth get an abortion! They threated to inform, Elizabeth's mother, robbed her of her self-esteem and self-worth, slandered the character of who she thought was.

She was made to feel less than nothing in their eyes. Deemed not suitable for them, she was judge for only what they saw on the outside. For hours, Jacob's parent ridiculed her to no ends, and blamed her for messing up Jacob's future.

Elizabeth looked over at Jacob, as he silently watched the continuous flow of Elizabeth's tears fall from her face.

The pain from a broken heart crippled Elizabeth, as she was tried to grasp everything that was happening. How could he just stand there and let this happen to her? Was this a dream, that she couldn't wake from? Did he really even love her?

The pain was more than unbearable and rage begin to set in. The last words Elizabeth heard was This way just a little and nothing more. My son will be going to college and this will be thing of the past. For a brief minute, everything in Elizabeth world begin to turned black and her body became numb to cope.

Elizabeth was alone and Jacob was an imposter in their love tringle.

Alone, Elizabeth fumbled her way to her car, blinded by her tears. She waited for just a little while, hoping Jacob would come running after her. Broken from the countless disappointments in one day, she headed home.

Chapter 3

Awoken by the fear of what laid ahead of her, Elizabeth felt lost and alone. Elizabeth feared her mother Pearl and did want to suffer her wrath.

But most important, Elizabeth couldn't bare the thought of Pearl looking at her with eyes filled with disappointment. Elizabeth worked hard to have her approval and everyone else she encountered.

But she would soon learn a lesson that she will never forget. Trying to please everyone is a full-time job and it becomes overwhelming, exhausting and soon it will cause you to mentally explode. Nevertheless, Elizabeth's mother Pearl was an extremely strict authoritarian. She was stern and harsh with her discipline. This made talking to her and telling her she might be pregnant even harder. Elizabeth remembers, when her older sister Caroline got pregnant and next thing she knew,

Chapter 3

Caroline was out of the house. Elizabeth could remember her mother and older sister always yelling. fighting and arguing.

Elizabeth was frightened by her thoughts, she had nowhere to go and no one to turn to for help. In that instant of her fragile state of mind, Elizabeth made the hardest decision of her young adult life. Elizabeth felt, she had no choice. Forged under pressure, she decidedto give in to Jacobs parents' wishes. Elizabeth had grown up in church and deep down inside, she knew it was wrong, but what other options did she have. There was nowhere to go and no other human being that she felt she could trust.

The screams for answers haunted her from the inside; Where was her help? Who could she turn to? Elizabeth's mother just couldn't find out and that was it.

She kept her feeling bottled up inside, never surfacing to the outside. Elizabeth smile on the outside as her pain demanded to be felt on the inside.

Elizabeth's state of mind was not healthy, for herself or anyone else.

Deep in thought, Elizabeth was awakened by the sound of medal clinging. Her cell doors had shut, and reality had set in again. As the prison guards

The Long Road Ahead

came around, to do count, she heard the quite voice of her roommate, a pregnant fair skinned lady say; "Do you mind me asking what are you in for?". With a long pause before answering, Elizabeth realized she didn't have an answer. With a look of confusion Elizabeth shrugged her shoulders as her eyes filled with tears.

Hey, it will be alright it's nothing permanent, Elizabeth roommate said with a gentle smile. Those words and that gentle smile somehow encouraged Elizabeth that day and for the first time she felt a glimpse of hope.

Chapter 4

Elizabeth smiled and closed her eyes, as her mind slipped back to the day when all was lost. It was the day of the abortion. It was a clear early Sunday morning; Elizabeth was nervous about fabricating a story, so she could make her appointment. Her heart was pounding, but it worked. Elizabeth had lied to her mom and told her that she needed help with a school project and would be home a little later than usual. On the drive to Jacob house, Elizabeth's nerves became more prudent, fear and anxiety stepped in. Something inside of her wanted to turn around and head for then hills. Elizabeth was afraid of the unknown, what she had to do made more sense, than running away to nothing. She finally arrived at Jacobs place. Elizabeth sat in her car for a few minutes, trying to make herself wake up from this nightmare. If she could just turn back time. After taking in a long deep breath, Elizabeth, suppressed her feelings and slowly made her way to Jacob's front door. She rang the doorbell

The Long Road Ahead

and Jacob's dad answered the door. With no concerns of how Elizabeth felt, he apathetically, said come in and yelled for Jacob to come downstairs.

Elizabeth stood in the living room with her head hand low, as Jacob came down the stairs. She looked up for just a second, to get a glimpse of Jacob's mother, standing at the top of the stairs. It looked like she had tears in her eyes and wanted to speak, but she never said a word.

Jacob's mom stayed behind and Elizabeth became confused as to why Jacob's dad was coming with them.

Jacob and Elizabeth got in the car and for some odd reason Jacob's dad followed behind them in his car.

Jacob and Elizabeth were on their way as Jacob's dad followed slowly behind them. Jacob and Elizabeth had not talked since that day of trauma. It was quite at first, only the words from the radio filled then atmosphere. Laughter broke the silence, something funny had been spoken on the radio and they laughed so hard. Jacob and Elizabeth talked and laughed the whole ride, never mentioning what laid before them.

Elizabeth allowed herself to forget what this day was truly about and her mind shifted to what was

Chapter 4

good. Her reality was distorted and she cling to the happiness she felt in that moment.

The ride seemed long, Elizabeth's excitement of being out of town was one of the distractions for her reality. Finally, after a couple hours or so, they had reached the destination. Elizabeth and Jacob slowly entered the building, still with Jacob's dad following slowly behind them.

They signed in and Elizabeth still didn't realize what laid ahead for her, until her named was called and she enter alone the doors of no return.

Chapter 5

The nurse prepared Elizabeth for the procedure, Elizabeth sat on the cold table and it hit her like a Mack truck.

The tears begin to fall and mind begin to race out of control. Elizabeth felt like she was spinning and she felt nauseated. It all hit her at once, she realized the tragedy of what was about to happen. The voices in her head were loud, overwhelming and she felt like she could not catch her breath. The doctor entered the room and began to start the procedure.

He introduced himself and turned around to Elizabeth and said "wow you're not even that far along, am surprised the test showed a positive result, but "don't worry it will all be over before you know it." Elizabeth never even took a test, she just assumed she was pregnant. It was so real now; Elizabeth didn't want to go through with it. She

Chapter 5

just couldn't, she felt trapped and with everything building up inside of her. At that very moment, she lost her control. Elizabeth jumped off the exam table and ran as fast as her feet could carry her, trying to find her way out. Blinded by her tears, she made her way back to the waiting room and jump right into Jacob's arms. Thinking she would be safe and he would take her away from this nightmare. Elizabeth held on to Jacob and wept historically.

Jacob's heart was beating fast and she felt his embrace. She wanted to go home, to be comforted, to find shelter from this storm.

Mortified by the voice she heard next, the voice of Jacob's dad as he uttered the words, she would soon never forget "Son get a handle that, we are not leaving until it is finished". Jacob's dad left after he said those knife stabbing words. Enraged with so much anger, so much pain and the shame of it all.

Elizabeth cried even harder, but it got her nowhere.

Elizabeth was alone and far away from home. It seemed that everyone had control over her life, but her. No one cared about what she was feeling and how deeply broken she really was. Elizabeth had no voice and no One could hear her screams from for help. At that moment she lost loss her joy and peace from within. Elizabeth barreled her head and

The Long Road Ahead

to Jacob's chest in hopes that he would save her. Jacob had allowed fear to overtake him and with tears in his eyes, he never said a word.

At that moment, Elizabeth's mind took her to a place of safety. The next voice she heard was the nurse saying "Miss it's going to be okay, come with me." The nurse gently pried Elizabeth From Jacob's lap and they slowly walked back to the procedure room.

Chapter 6

The pure white snow fell to the ground, as Elizabeth gazed out the window covered with bars. After being in prison for a couple of days, all she could think about was being home. Awakened from her daze, Elizabeth was startled by the guard yelling church in 10 minutes. Elizabeth jumped up and rushed toward the line.

Elizabeth always enjoyed going to church, especially as a little girl.

In fact, going to church always seemed to give her a sense of peace, a glimpse of hope and it just felt safe and Elizabeth loved to sing. Plus, anywhere was better then, starring at the same four walls all-day. In a single file Elizabeth and the other inmates arrived to a larger room, with a few chairs and a podium.

The Long Road Ahead

Elizabeth and the other inmates singed along with the officials. For a split moment Elizabeth found a hint of joy. After two songs, the Lady Pastor opened up with a prayer and begin to speak. "Our past does not define who we are". Those were the only words Elizabeth heard, before her mind drifted back to the captivity of her past. The sound of clapping woke Elizabeth from her trance-like state. When she looked up, the service was coming to a close. The pastor closed the Bible and offered prayer to anyone who wanted it. Elizabeth was determined to find some peace from the constant battles that took place in her mind.

She stood up and made her way to the front and tears begin to rolled down her face. Elizabeth could not control her emotions as she stood in line. She was next, as she moved forward towards the Pastor; the paster, just starred at Elizabeth, as if she could see through her very soul.

She looked into Elizabeth's brown eyes. They were filled with so much pain, shame, regret and disappointment. The pastor white Elizabeth's tears and gave her a nurturing smile, which caused Elizabeth to chuckle and smile back.

The pastor leaned over closer to Elizabeth and whispered sweetly, in a powerful voice filled with hope and love, ten words aroused Elizabeth's inner

Chapter 6

spirit man! She said "Most favored and anointed one of God, this is not your end, only the beginning". Elizabeth felt a whirlwind of peace overtake her and her and instantly, she drifted into a calm encounter wrapped in God's love.

After that day Elizabeth had felt an unexplainable hunger, one that natural food could not satisfy. In a few days Elizabeth would soon face trial, to determine her fate.

From that day forward the days felt long and the people strange, but Elizabeth felt that everything was going to work out in her favor.

Chapter 7

The day was coming to an end and Elizabeth was tired from trying to stay up to keep herself busy. Elizabeth felt that everything would be all right, but her mind was clouded with the many voices filled her head. Elizabeth knew that her life was in the hands of the judge that she would soon stand in front of.

The guard yelled "lights out in 5." Elizabeth jumped on to her top bunk and laid her head down on the uncomfortable pillow. Her eyes begin to drift shut and she woke up in the recovery room of the abortion clinic. Elizabeth heard the voice of the nurse calling her name. Elizabeth; " wake up dear, it's all done, the procedure went well". Elizabeth slowly opened her eyes. She was confused and drowsy from the sedation. The nurse vaguely read the discharge instruction. Elizabeth felt empty, ashamed and tears flooded her eyes. "Everything's all right"

Chapter 7

said the nurse, as she helped Elizabeth prepare to go home.

Walking out to the waiting room seemed like the hardest task, every step seemed to be longer than the first. Elizabeth looked around the waiting room.

There was no sign of Jacob's dad. Jacob sat there waiting, as the nurse released Elizabeth into his care. Not knowing what to except, Jacob had a look of sorrowful regret, across his face and the only words, he could mustard up to say was, "you had me sacred for a moment. Elizabeth just smiled a little, shook her head and they headed towards the exit. The car ride home was tense and silent and not a word spoken. It was like they were strangers riding together. You could actually hear a pin drop. A dark cloud of emptiness hovered over Elizabeth's lifeless body as she blankly gazed out the car window.

The car ride back to Jacob's house, seemed much shorter this time and before they knew it the car had come to a stop and suddenly their journey had ended. Jacob waited for Elizabeth to get out the car. He gave a short hug and they said their good byes. Elizabeth felt dead inside, but she was smiling on the outside. She felt as if she was outside her body watching all these events occur. Elizabeth walked

The Long Road Ahead

slowly towards her car, feeling the demanding pain from the procedure.

The drive home seemed longer than all the drives before that day. Elizabeth could hardly see the road from the tears that constantly flowed from her eyes. The pain from within kept demanding to be felt and Elizabeth pulled over and screamed from the top of her lungs, she wanted to crawl in a hole and die.

It was all too unbearable, but she knew if she didn't make it home in time, she would be in even more trouble.

So, Elizabeth quickly wiped her eyes, pulled herself together and before she knew it, she was pulling into the driveway of her mother's house. She took one deep breath after another, as she put on a smile and walked into the house, as if nothing ever happened. No one was downstairs and her younger sister Ashley and younger brother Nathan were visiting with their friends. Elizabeth was relieved, she just wanted to rest and put this day behind her. Elizabeth slowly made her way upstairs, feeling the painful effects from the procedure. When she reached the top in anguish. She heard the voice of her mother call out, " is that you Elizabeth? Yes mom, it's me, Elizabeth answered, trying to hold back her tears.

Chapter 7

Elizabeth wanted so badly to run and jump in her mother's arms and tell her about the awful/ tragic thing that had happened to her.

Until she heard her mother say, " I have to work tonight; I don't want any noise. Did you eat yet? There's food on the stove if you're hungry and make sure you put those dishes away." Yes mama, Elizabeth replied as she laid quietly on her bed and held her stuff animal tightly. Elizabeth tossed and turned, she wanted so badly to lie in her mother's arms for comfort and tell her everything, but she was afraid.

Chapter 8

The next morning was a school day and Elizabeth couldn't help but think she was in a nightmare trying to wake up. Her post-procedure instructions called for rest, but she couldn't. Elizabeth had to go to school, like nothing happened. It was the only way to keep her secret from being revealed at home. The pain she felt that morning from the procedure made everything so real. Elizabeth and her little sister Ashley got ready for school. Elizabeth had no appetite and her mind was racing with many thoughts. Who knew? Who did he tell?

How could she face Jacob and the shame of what happen? School was no longer one of Elizabeth's favorite places to be. The thought of seeing Jacob made her stomach churn. Elizabeth tried hard to hold herself together on the drive to school. She parked in the parking lot, then informed Ashley she was leaving early and she would have to catch the bus.

Chapter 8

Elizabeth stayed behind for a few minutes and closed her eyes tightly, trying to contain the pain she felt from inside and the pain from the procedure.

Life was moving on, while she was stayed stuck in her world of physical and mental pain. Elizabeth pulled herself together and slowly walked toward the front doors of the school building.

She could hear the gossip, the snickering and feel the piercing stares as she walked through the halls to her first period. Elizabeth wanted to crawl into a hole and just never come out, but she masked her feelings with a smile, held her head high and finished out the day.

No one really said anything to her face, even Elizabeth so called friends at that time, never really uttered a word. It was like there was a huge elephant in the room that no one wanted to address.

When the bell rang Elizabeth felt a sense of relief, home never look so good. Elizabeth was the middle child of two brother and two sisters. Only her younger sister Ashly and younger brother Nathan lived with her at home. Elizabeth's younger sister Ashely came home acting stranger than usual. She was ruder than usual, very drawn back and seemed agitated by Elizabeth's presence. Elizabeth and Ashley didn't have the greatest sisterly relationship, so Elizabeth just ignored her, she had other things

The Long Road Ahead

to worry about. Their mom was working a double and would soon be home. Elizabeth started to do her chores and Ashley kept making smart remarks to agitate her.

Elizabeth started to wash the dishes. Ashley was busy talking on the phone with a friend and neglecting her chores. Elizabeth was really frustrated with Ashley's behavior, she asked her to hurry up with her phone call. Ashley looked at Elizabeth and hang up the phone with a sassy attitude.

Elizabeth couldn't take it any longer, they begin to argue, it was nothing new under the sun. But what Ashley said next, cut Elizabeth deep like a two-edged sword. "I hate you and everybody knows about your stupid abortion; you're a real whore and the whole school knows it." Ashley laughed, as those words ripped right though Elizabeth heart, and something snapped on the inside. Elizabeth was at her breaking point and she blackout. Blinded by her own rage, she grabbed a butter knife and throw it across the room towards Ashley, she couldn't stop. Elizabeth was out of control, screaming and crying from the hurt that lie inside. Many feelings crowded her mind and she ran up to her room. Trying to seek comfort in her favorite stuff animal, she curled up in a ball and tightly closed her eyes. Everything was dark and Elizabeth laid there, trying to calm the battlefield in her mind.

Chapter 9

A loud forceful knock on the door startled Elizabeth, but she was numb and couldn't move. The voice of a man yelled from downstairs. "It's the police come out with your hands where we can see them. Everything was happening so fast, Elizabeth felt yourself spinning in circles of doom and despair.

Clueless of what was transpiring right under her nose. She felt a presence in her room as her lifeless body laid terrified of what was next to come.

"Show me your hands", yelled the officers in an aggressive and harsh voice. Elizabeth turned over slowly with tears in her eyes, shocked, as she starred down the barrel of the officer's guns. Elizabeth was confused, trying to figure out what was happening and why there were two police officers in her room. Darkness overcame Elizabeth heart, as the officers roughly stood her up and cuff her hands behind

The Long Road Ahead

her back. They drag Elizabeth down the stairs, because she was drain from the storm, that had tormented her very existence. There was no energy left to give in her body. On the way out to the car, Elizabeth heard the voice of her mother screaming. "O Lord! What is going on here and why is she in hand cuffs. Wait just a minute, I only called you to calm her down until I arrive home." The officer stated, Ma'am we will be escorting her to the psychiatric ward to be evaluated treated. Then, after her treatment, she will be charged with assault with a deadly weapon and intent to cause bodily harm to a minor.

When the officer shut the door to the police car, Elizabeth was awakened out of her nightmare, by the voice the prison guard yelling; "showers ladies and then line up for chowtime. Elizabeth reality had set in once again. At that very moment, Elizabeth realized that the love that she thought she needed, cost her everything and the choices she made resulted in her imprisonment.

Chapter 10

The sun shined brightly that cold winter morning, as Elizabeth rose for her bunk. It was the day of her trial.

She was excited about possibly being released and going home, but she also feared the unknown.

Elizabeth was not only about to find out if she would be going home, but she also had to face her reality once again. She was the girl who got pregnant and had an abortion and then a nervous breakdown, which led to her imprisonment. This was it, Elizabeth prepared herself mentally and physically the best way she knew how. The guard called for all the inmates with court papers to check-in and line-up. Elizabeth couldn't help herself, her anxiety kicked in as she and the other prisoners lined up to board the bus going to the courthouse. She could not control her thoughts; they were racing and her emotions were everywhere. All Elizabeth

The Long Road Ahead

knew was that, she did not want to come back to this place. Trying to hold back her tears, Elizabeth got on the bus and took her seat. Elizabeth had not seen anyone since the incident, not even her own family. It was a month of loneliness and she missed them all. They were her family and nothing could ever change that. The ride to the courthouse from the prison seemed extremely long. Elizabeth didn't realize how far away from home she really was. She closed her eyes, laid her head on the window and tried to calm her emotions and before she knew it, they were stopping in front of the courthouse. Elizabeth and the other inmates were assisted off the bus and into the building by the guards. Walking into the courthouse shackled and chains, Elizabeth felt embarrassed and ashamed, and even more so, after seeing her mother, Pearl. Elizabeth and the other inmates were locked back up into a smaller prison, as they waited their turn for arraignment.

Walking into the courtroom Elizabeth felt sick to her stomach. She stood in front of the Judge. After hours of anticipation, Elizabeth's name was finally called, to appear before the Judge. Walking into the courtroom Elizabeth felt sick to her stomach. She stood in front of the Judge. He viewed her case and then looked up at Elizabeth and asked her, "How do you plea? young lady." With knots in her stomach and her eyes filled with tears, Elizabeth

Chapter 10

muttered the words "Guilty." Elizabeth took a deep breath and hung her head low, to accept her fate. The Judge ordered 6 months' probation and for Elizabeth to be returned to her mother. Elizabeth couldn't believe, she started crying. She was thankful was filled with joy and excitement. Elizabeth was pardon from her captivity and she was going home.

Elizabeth was happy and grateful to be going home. But the fear of the unknown overwhelmed her, as they prepared her to be released to her mother Pearl. Questions filled her head; What would she say to her mother? How would her mom react to seeing her? How was Ashley? Will she be able to catch up with her school work? Did she still have friends? What next and who knew?

Elizabeth felt ashamed when she stood before her mother. She was a teenage being released from prison. They hugged and made their way to the car. "How are you doing?" her mother said. "I'm glad to be going home", Elizabeth replied trying to hold back her tears of feeling like a complete disappointment. The ride home was quiet after that and not much was said.

When they arrived home. When they arrive home, there was no welcome party. Ashley and her younger brother Nathan were still in school.

The Long Road Ahead

Elizabeth went straight to her room and laid on her bed. Everything was like she left it; quiet, spotless and everything in its in proper place. Pearl, had to work that night, so she started dinner and later went to lay down. A legacy of secrets and unspoken words were our family strong suit.

"When past hurts and pain are buried, they usually are forced to the surface and erupt like an explosive volcano."

The day dragged on, no visitors, nothing, just the same routine. No one really said much, but things were definitely different. When Elizabeth finally got to see her sister and brother, she was glad to see them, but no one really addressed the enormous elephant that was in the room.

The next morning was a school day and Elizabeth couldn't afford to miss any more days. Plus, staying home was not an option. She was tired from a sleepless night of tossing and turning, but she got ready and headed off to school. Ashley had caught the bus early that morning. Their relationship was already not the greatest, but it was now, in need of some major repair.

She started up her car and before she knew it, she was in the school parking lot. Elizabeth felt short of breath and begin to feel the anxiety of facing everyone. Startled by a knock on her window, she

Chapter 10

noticed her good friend Laura waiting for her to get out. Walking through the school halls reminded her of the day of the abortion. The stares were piercing and the snickering was loud.

Elizabeth wanted to run and hide under a rock. Laura stayed by her side as they walked to their first period class. It was Elizabeth's senior year and she had a lot to caught up on. Everything was so overwhelming and seeing Jacob made everything ten times worse. Elizabeth felt like a stranger and her own hometown. Time was moving forward, but she was the only one standing still. The bell rang and it was lunch time, Elizabeth didn't have much of an appetite. She slipped her water, while noticing an average size Caucasian male staring intensely at her from the corner of her eyes.

She could only guess what he was thinking about, what everyone was thinking. The lunch room was filled with loud chatter and Elizabeth's shame showed as she sat in silence. Hearing the bell ring was relieving and Elizabeth quickly made her way to her next class. Elizabeth couldn't concentrate, the battlefield and her mind was piercing. She raised her hand and got a pass to go to the bathroom. When Elizabeth got to the bathroom, she splashed water on her face her face to help with the anxiety. After she got herself together, Elizabeth decided to walk around for a while before she headed it

The Long Road Ahead

back. This was not typical behavior for Elizabeth, but Elizabeth was different. Startled by the presence of a teacher in the hall, Elizabeth turned to hurry back to class. As, she turned the corner, she saw him, the boy from the lunch room.

Their eyes met and he kept staring at her. Then he called out to her, in a deep voice, "Hey shorty." Elizabeth giggled at his boyish actions, then she waved for him to come meet her in the hall. He was in study hall so it was easy for him to get a pass. Elizabeth had no clue what she was doing. She knew he was wasn't good for her, he was a wild bad boy, with no intentions of following the rules. They walked around and talked for a while. He made her laugh in a girlish way. His name was Jason and Elizabeth found out that, he had a major crush on her. He was not shy and he wanted Elizabeth. With his deep voice, boyish behavior and multicolored eyes, it hard for Elizabeth to say no! Without even thinking Elizabeth gave him her number and hurried read back to class.

The day was finally over and Elizabeth's sighed in relief. She walked swiftly to her car and drove straight home. She had a rough day, but as she recalled, her meeting with Jason, it made her smile.

Elizabeth got home and tackled her chores, before hitting the mountains of make-up work, she had.

Chapter 10

Her mother Pearl, was finishing up dinner. They had a brief conversation, about Elizabeth's day. Everyone was getting home from school and they sat down to have dinner as a family. Afterwards, Pearl went to lay down and rest a little before work. Elizabeth tackled the dinner dishes and got started on her school work. Time was flying fast; Elizabeth's mom had got ready and left for work. Jason still had not called and it was getting late. Feeling dishearten, Elizabeth got ready for bed. As, laid down to close her eyes, the phone. Elizabeth rush downstairs! "Hello!" It was Jason on the other line! His voice was deep and soft and it gave her chills. She couldn't believe he called; she was happy. He was the first person, that was a distraction from her storm.

They talked for hours; it was almost nearing the morning when they ended the call. She had been struck by his charm and the next day Elizabeth met Jason in the parking lot. They walked into the building his hand and hers.

They were together and now everyone knew it. The bell rang and Jason pulled Elizabeth close, to softly kiss her lips. They went their separate ways. Elizabeth couldn't believe he kissed her, they just met! Her world was spinning fast, but it felt nice to be wanted. So, Elizabeth accepted what was and took a chance on love again. In the middle of class,

The Long Road Ahead

Elizabeth was called down to the principles officer. Her stomach churned, as she made her way down to the office.

The principle had informed her that her probation had sent over paperwork stating that she was not to have contact with her younger sister Ashley for 6 months or until cleared by her probation.

This was the first time Elizabeth heard of this order. She and her sister Ashley attended the same school and lived together. Elizabeth's heart began to race! It was starting again, "The nightmare". Elizabeth was in her senior year and she could not believe what she was hearing. It seemed like every time she was moving forward, out of nowhere appeared a roadblock. Elizabeth could not hold back her tears, as she left the office. Her heart was filled with despair and the outcome weighed heavily on her shoulders. She walked the halls, feeling defeated by her past. Elizabeth couldn't bear to face her mother with this terrible news, so much had already put them in a place of distance. Elizabeth walked past her English teacher class. Mr. Lambert came out and asked if she had a pass and Elizabeth begin to cry. Mr. Lambert pulled her to the side and asked what was going on. Elizabeth began to pour out her hurt, the pain and shame from the abortion and now not being able to finish out the year. She was devastated and quit a mess. Mr. Lambert offered

Chapter 10

Elizabeth a tissue and a glimpse of hope, as he walked her back to the principal office. Lambert acted, as if he was Elizabeth's guardian angel. She was on trial and he stepped in as her lawyer.

Elizabeth set back in awe, as she watched Mr. Lambert defended and stood up for her. When he finished up, Elizabeth's face filled with joy, as they made a decision to allow her to graduate, with her fellow students.

Elizabeth was thankful for what Mr. Lambert had done for her and she wondered why he did. Inspiring, potential, strong, determined and brave were the words, he used to describe her.

Elizabeth was encouraged by Mr. Lambert's acts of kindness. She realized that not everyone was against her and seen the worst in her.

Just when we think it's the end of the road, God always sends help, in ways we would never have imagined. "Remember there's always more roads than road blocks."

Chapter 11

Graduation was finally here. Jason and Elizabeth were so in love and holding on strong. Jason was a year behind her, but they had plans to be together forever. Elizabeth had plans to go off to college, become a CNRNA and wait for Jason.

It was the day of graduation, Elizabeth was so excited and grateful to God, she had made it. She defeated the odds of the not so easy road she traveled.

It was windy the day of graduation and a little chilly as Elizabeth and her classmates marched onto the football field. Elizabeth had knots in her stomach and felt a little nauseous. Must be nerves she thought, as she patiently waited for her name to be called. It was finally Elizabeth turn and she jumped up with smiles of enthusiasm and anxiously walked onto the stage to receive her high

Chapter 11

school diploma. In excitement, while returning to her seat, Elizabeth tripped over the wire on the ground. She barely caught herself, as the crowd giggled. Elizabeth was as giddy and clumsy as they came.

After graduation, Elizabeth went home to celebrate with her family. Overwhelmed by all the excitement, Elizabeth headed upstairs to lay down a bit. High school was over, and Elizabeth was looking forward to going to college, but the thought of leaving Jason behind terrified her. Later that evening, Elizabeth and her friend Amy went out to some after parties. Elizabeth still felt sick, but she went anyway. They were high school graduates and the parties were live. They tried to visit them all. They socialized and danced for a while and to the next party they went.

Elizabeth tried to catch some ZZ's in between, the bed was where she really wanted to be. Soon they met up with Jason and Elizabeth jumped into his arms and they hugged, as if they hadn't seen one another for years.

He was happy for her as he presented her with a flower. Being sweet was not one of Jason's strong suits, but every now and then he would surprise her. Elizabeth sat in Jason lap most of the night as they mingled with friends. Everything was perfect,

The Long Road Ahead

but it was getting late. Elizabeth had a curfew and she had no intentions of seeing what would happen to her it she broke it. Jason and Elizabeth sealed the night with a kiss and said their good byes.

Amy took Elizabeth home and Elizabeth couldn't wait to take a long shower and get in her nice warm bed. Jason called to check on her, they talked for a while and then Elizabeth headed for bed.

The morning came quickly and Elizabeth felt like she had been hit by a Mack truck.

The flu, it must be the flu she thought, so she made a doctor's appointment. Elizabeth laid around all day awaiting to go to the doctors.

She was miserable couldn't eat or drink and had a headache and stomachache straight from hell. The time had finally come and Elizabeth couldn't wait to get some relief. The waiting room was full, there had to be something going around.

The nurse called Elizabeth back and took her vitals and documented her symptoms into the computer. The nurse looked up from her computer and asked Elizabeth; Do you think you could be pregnant? Elizabeth had no words; the thought had never crossed Elizabeth mind. Elizabeth scratched head, shrugged her shoulders and laughed, as she replied; of course not. Well, we will urine a sample. The

Chapter 11

nurse handed Elizabeth a collecting cup and she walked slowly to the bathroom, trying to remember the last time she and Jason were intimate. She returned from the bathroom and waited for the nurse to return. There was a knock on the door and the doctor entered. She greeted Elizabeth and then begin to make documentation on the computer. Elizabeth's mind and heart begin to race. She took in a deep breath and just as she exhaled, the doctor turned turn to her and said "Thankfully you do not have the flu, but you are about six weeks pregnant. Elizabeth looked at her with a face of confusion. Then she blurted out, this cannot be happening; not again. The doctor comforted her and informed her of her options and the help that was available. Elizabeth only heard every other word, as she remembered her and Jason's careless night of passion.

Elizabeth stared blankly at the wall. She had a hard time processing what the doctor said. In denial of what was said, she asked "what kind of anti-biotics will I need to take.

With a concerned look on her face, the doctor repeated her diagnosis, no dear it's not the flu. You are with child! Realizing what was really said, Elizabeth heart filled fear and her eyes filled with tears.

The Long Road Ahead

On the long lonely ride home Elizabeth wandered how was she going to tell Jason and her mother. She was afraid to tell either of them. When Elizabeth got home her mother was sleep from a long night at work. She immediately called Jason, she had to know his thoughts. Jason was still in bed, but Elizabeth insisted that she needed to talk to him and he made his way over to her. She didn't tell him right away, she just wanted to get out the house. While they were driving to Jason house, Elizabeth just handed him the results without a word. Jason turned and looked at Elizabeth with a look of confusion. Before he could say anything, Jason had run into the back of the car in front of him. Immediately he jumped out to go check on Elizabeth. She was shocked from the impact, but she was fine. The accident was not as bad, as the impact felt. The police came and assessed the accident and tickets were issued. It was quick and hardly any damage occurred on either side. Jason and Elizabeth were lucky, they were able to drive home. After the accident, the ride to Jason's house was awkward. It was silent for a brief moment, then Jason asked Elizabeth, what she wanted to do. Elizabeth heart filled with fear and she turned to Jason and screamed: I'm not going to get an abortion! Then she began to cry hysterically. They pulled into the driveway. Jason turned to Elizabeth in confusion and rubbed her back.

Chapter 11

He assured her, that was not what he was asking. In a deep and soothing voice, he said; "I would never ask that of you unless it was what you wanted". Elizabeth began to feel a sense of calmness. He wiped her eyes and she took a deep breath and smiled in embarrassment of her reactions. "If we don't deal with the skeletons in our past, they will always find a way into our future".

I have to tell my parents he said, and all Elizabeth could think of was the ridicule she might endure. Elizabeth had met Jason's parents before. She loved them both, they had their ways but they accepted her. Jason told his parents as they stood together hand-in-hand. Elizabeth thought she would just faint, she could not endure any more heartbreak. Jason's mother Mary was thrilled and came over and gave Elizabeth a loving hug and a smile of reassurance. This time was different.

John, Jason's dad, on the other hand did not look so happy. He was sterner and quite disappointed. He had a lot of questions and he wanted answers. What were their plans? and how do they plan to take care of a baby? Elizabeth and Jason had no clue of how to answer any of his questions, all they knew was that they loved each other and the rest they would have to figure it out as it came. Elizabeth just had to figure out how she was going to tell her mother. Jason and Elizabeth spent the

The Long Road Ahead

day together. They talked about marriage, school, getting their own place and of course, their bundle of joy that that was growing inside of her.

It was like a dream, but the reality was the reality was Elizabeth had just graduated and both of them lived at home with their parents.

Jason was still in high school and the reality of it all was quite overwhelming, when she really thought it through. The thought of how Mom Pearl would react to the news, made Elizabeth nauseous. Later that afternoon Jason dropped Elizabeth off at home. They sat in the car for a few minutes and Elizabeth explained to him that telling her mom was something she needed to do alone. Jason had a look of co fusion, but he respected her wishes. Elizabeth waved by to Jason and then she paced up and down the sidewalk. There was no good way or good time to tell her mother. "No time or way seemed good to spare a fight today and die tomorrow". Elizabeth took a deep breath and she went to speak with her mother. Pearl was upstairs in her room watching Tv. Elizabeth knocks on the door and enter. Elizabeth got right to it while she still had the nerves. Pearl listened to Elizabeth's every word. Elizabeth voice trembled, as she stared into her mother's face, that was lit with disappointment. When Elizabeth finished explaining to her mother about the pregnancy, her knees became weak. Pearl just kept shaking her

Chapter 11

head, then she got up, threw her hands in the air and scolded Elizabeth harshly and ordered out of her sight. Elizabeth tried her best not to cry as she realized her mother expected better of her and she was disappointed in her careless actions. Elizabeth held her head down low and walked back to her room. Pearl slammed her door and there was nothing but silence. Elizabeth felt trapped in the pit of despair and shame. She had let her mother down and the secret from before was still untold. Later that evening Elizabeth heard her mother getting ready for work. She was afraid of facing her and enduring what she might say, but there were no words exchanged. Pearl walked downstairs, the door shut and Elizabeth's mom was gone.

Chapter 12

Elizabeth was nine months into her pregnancy and still living at home.

Juggling work and school were exhausting and with the daily attitudes from her sister Ashley, it didn't make life any easier. Elizabeth and her mother were starting to have a better relationship and Elizabeth did whatever possible to keep it that way.

Jason and Elizabeth were still hanging tuff. Jason was in his senior year, with three more months until graduation. Early that morning at work Elizabeth began to have contractions, they came and they went. Work seemed to drag that day and Elizabeth couldn't wait to go home. when Elizabeth arrived home that afternoon her mother had set some dinner aside for her. She warmed it up and set down and ate. Everything was delicious, but she kept feeling a sharp pain. Elizabeth went to

Chapter 12

the bathroom and let out a loud screech. Elizabeth mother came flying down the stairs to find Elizabeth crying on the bathroom floor. Elizabeth was in labor! Pearl got the bags ready, called the doctor and they headed off to the hospital. Elizabeth tried to reach Jason, but he was not answering.

The contractions were stronger and longer as they got closer to the hospital.

Pearl helped Elizabeth as they walked in the hospital. They got on the elevator and went straight to the labor and delivery floor. Elizabeth was in a lot of pain but she tried her best to be brave. When they arrive to the labor and delivery floor, Elizabeth got checked in and the nurse helped her get settled in. By the time Jason made it to the hospital, Elizabeth was already prepped with an IV and close to delivery. Friends and family filled the birthing room. Elizabeth was fully dilated and it was time to push. She was trying her best not to act the way she felt. The pain was excruciating but, Elizabeth was used to keeping her screams in the inside.

Everyone was being encouraging, but it was irritating to Elizabeth and she made everyone get out. Only her mother, Jason and his mother remained. Elizabeth was overwhelmed by all the yelling, the talking, the pushing and the pain. Buildup from the pain, her surroundings and everyone was

The Long Road Ahead

starting to spill over. Elizabeth wanted to give up. She couldn't take much more and then it happened! Jason Made a comment that really wasn't all that bad. Elizabeth had just, had enough of everyone telling her how she felt. Jason giggled a little and said "come on babe, it can't hurt that bad". Elizabeth turned towards him with fire in her eyes and before you knew it she had slapped Jason right across the face. The room went silent and the doctor suggested, everyone take a moment.

The room was silent, as the doctor resumed with the labor process. I need you to push Elizabeth, said the doctor. Elizabeth closed her eyes to block out everything that had happened and she gave a big push and the baby's head came out. Excitement filled the room and Elizabeth laid back and relief. She was tired and had no energy. She began drifting off to sleep as she watched everyone smiling with tears of joy. Elizabeth thought it was over.

Until, worry filled the room, as the doctor yelled, "he's turning purple I need you to push. Elizabeth began to cry; she was so weak as she looked over at her mother.

Pearl grabbed Elizabeth's hand and said with a look of distress " you have to push baby!" Pearl helped Elizabeth up and rubbed her back. Elizabeth grabbed her knees and bared down with all she

Chapter 12

had. The baby was out, and tears of joy spread across the room. Noah was finally here and as the nurse placed him on her chest Elizabeth smiled at the little miracle given by God. The next day, reality hit hard. Elizabeth and Jason were parents. They were responsible for this little person, who needed them. The thought of it scared Elizabeth. She didn't feel that she would be enough for him. They had a lot of visitors from friends and family. Elizabeth was Elizabeth was drawn back from it all, trying to figure out how to be no Noah's mother. Soon it would be time to go home and Elizabeth would be on her own. Jason and Elizabeth still didn't have their own place and Elizabeth shared a room with her younger sister. On top of all of that, Elizabeth had no clue of how to raise a baby and especially be someone's mother. "How do you give someone love when you don't even know what love is yourself?" The days seemed shorter and the nights seemed longer now that Noah was here.

Elizabeth younger sister was frustrated and didn't like that fact that she had to share a room with Elizabeth and a baby. Therefore, she made living there a living hell for Elizabeth, with every chance she could get. Elizabeth tried to spend most of her days outside, so she didn't bother anyone, especially when Noah cried.

The Long Road Ahead

One morning, Grace and old friend came over to visit with Elizabeth and see Noah. They talked and laughed they had been friends for years just never really hang out.

Before leaving Grace invited Elizabeth and Noah to church. Elizabeth agreed, she had missed church and her mother really go didn't go anymore. The thought of going to church again excited Elizabeth she couldn't wait, especially to get away from the turmoil and unspoken words in the house. Sunday came fast and Elizabeth and Noah were dressed and ready. Elizabeth felt a since of peace as they pulled into the church parking lot.

She could hear the music playing from the outside! Music made Elizabeth happy and she loved to sing. She walked in and it felt like home. The atmosphere stirred up something deep inside of her and it felt good! Elizabeth had not felt that feeling in a long time. She felt fulfilled!

The service was uplifting and Elizabeth rededicated her life back to Christ. The days ahead tested her faith in her journey as a renewed Christian.

Chapter 13

Elizabeth had just graduated from her technical college and could no longer take the agony of being treated like an outsider by her household.

Jason and Elizabeth we're trying their best to spent time together and be parents. They had different lives and lived at different homes. Elizabeth was always complaining to Jason about everything she and Noah had to endure, living at her mom's house.

Jason wanted to make things better for Elizabeth and Noah, so he made provisions for the both of them to come live with him at his parent's house.

Elizabeth wanted her own place, but could not afford it. She was grateful for Jason's parents letting her and Noah stay with them, but she didn't like it one bit. She had no privacy and Jason's mother Mary, was always there wanting to help and give advice. She meant well and this was her

The Long Road Ahead

first grandbaby. She was sweet, loving and practically amazing. But it was hard to raise Noah with someone always over your shoulder and constantly trying to take over. Elizabeth was thankful and happy to have her there. In addition, mentally Elizabeth was dealing with everything and the transition, from her house to Jason's was a lot to take in. The constant advice and control of others made Elizabeth feel inadequate and a failure. It seemed, everyone had control over Elizabeth's life except her. She wanted to be good at something. Noah was her something and she wanted to be good for him. The atmosphere and Elizabeth's surroundings were different. It took some time to get used to. Mary and Elizabeth relationship grew a little stronger as the months went by. After Jason's graduation, Elizabeth lived with Jason and his parents for a few more months. Later, Elizabeth and Jason got there first apartment together! The beginning was wonderful and Elizabeth tried hard to make things between them work. She believed they loved each other, but the fast forward button had been pushed on their lives. They were young and they had a child, which put an unexpected strain on their relationship. Elizabeth had been through a lot, she was older and had a very mature mindset. She was ready to settle down and give Noah a life she never had. Jason on the other hand was younger and not so mature. He had changed when they got their own place. Smoking and drinking and staying

Chapter 13

out with friends a little more than usual. Jason had a family but, he showed no interest in settling down. He was caught up in illegal affairs and living a bachelor's life. Elizabeth knew he smoked marijuana and every so oftem, he would make a profit off of it.

She thought, Jason was just having a boyish high school phase. She hoped, that his behavior would change after they had Noah. Jason really enjoyed being Noah's father and he loved him. Jason was more involved than he led on. Elizabeth was starting to feel like a fly, that blindly run into a web of deception and disappointment. As the weeks went by, Jason became more and more obsessed with smoking, drinking and selling marijuana. Elizabeth tried to stay with him in hopes that he would come to his senses and choose his family. They argued a lot and disagreed on all most everything. Elizabeth really loved Jason dearly and wanted a life with him, but not at the expense of putting her and their son Noah in the face of danger. She had to think about Noah and their safety.

Chapter 14

Months went by and Elizabeth was miserable in her current situation and ready to call it quits. Out of the blue, Jason decided to try and reconcile things between the two of them. Jason had planned a nice trip to the beach. They were going on a date; it was the first in a while. Jason's parents watched Noah and kept him for the night. Elizabeth was excited they had not been alone together for a while; they could finally talk and hopefully work things out. Jason told Elizabeth, he had to make a stop before they headed out. They pulled up to a hidden road and drove up to a dirty, old white building.

Jacob looked over at Elizabeth and said, "I will be right back and he kissed her softly on the cheek.

Elizabeth smiled and waited patiently in the car. It was hot that day and Jason seemed to be taking forever. Elizabeth became impatient, so she got out of

Chapter 14

the car and went to the door where she saw Jason enter. She knocked softly and the door opened slowly. A thin, pale, sickly looking Caucasian female answered the door! Elizabeth was confused as her eyes pane around looking for Jason. Jason waved her to come in. Elizabeth was not sure what was going on, Jason informed her, he would just be a few more minutes. Elizabeth headed for the couch, unaware of what was transpiring right under her nose. Observing her surroundings, Elizabeth noticed a little baby boy in an off-white dirty bassinet, in the corner. Elizabeth began to feel uncomfortable; something didn't seem right and she wanted to leave. She tried to make eye contact with Jason. She moved to the middle of the couch so she could see him. When she finally got in his view, she couldn't believe what she was seeing. Jason; the man she loved, was standing at the stove cooking some type of drugs up, for the Caucasian female and the male who stayed hidden in the corner. Elizabeth was disgusted at what she had just witnessed. Her body went into shock as her mind tried to protect her from what was occurring. Who was this person she was looking at? Jason was like a stranger to her. Where was the boy she fell in love with? And who was this man who stood in front of her?

The Long Road Ahead

All Elizabeth could think of was the little baby in the corner and what would happen to him when they leave.

Elizabeth thoughts were overwhelming and she had to get out of there. She got up and ran to the car. Elizabeth couldn't catch her breath; she was having an anxiety attack! She fell to the ground and tried to catch her breath. Then, she looked around at her surroundings. She wanted to make a run for it but realized and realized she was stuck. Elizabeth had no clue of where she was. In that moment, she just stood up and brushed a dirt from her pants and got in the car. Jason finally came out and got in the car. Elizabeth was shaking with fear, of the man who sat beside her.

Jason started up the car and drove from that place. He said nothing, he acted if nothing had happened. There was a big fat elephant sitting in the car with them and he didn't acknowledge it. It was smothering Elizabeth and with a trembling voice; Elizabeth asked Jason to take her home now. Jason became irritated with Elizabeth. He pulled over; they argued a little. Why are you trying to ruin this day, Elizabeth? he shouted! Elizabeth begin to cry, her heart was broken and silence filled that car. Jason turned the care around and headed towards home. The car ride home seemed long and tensed. As they pulled into the driveway of their apartment

Chapter 14

complex, the build-up of anger and brokenness inside of her demanded to be felt. Elizabeth tried to hold in what she was truly feeling any longer.

She turned to Jason, with tears of frustration and betrayal. How could you and that poor baby. Who are you and why are you doing this to us she yelled?

Jason looked over at Elizabeth and she seen the monster within. Jason words were evil and heavy to hear, as he said, "It's their problem, their crackheads, no one cares about them".

It's their life and their business. Elizabeth was shocked at the way Jason responded. It was like talking to a wall. His heart was hardened and he had no sympathy of what had taken place. Elizabeth closed her eyes, as she began to feel the darkness from her shattered and broken heart take over. Her eyes were open and she could see clearly. The man that she loved, so dearly was a full- blown heartless drug dealer. Elizabeth's happily ever after was seen for what it really was; a distraction, to keep her down and broken. Elizabeth was paralyzed with the fear of the unknown once again. Elizabeth lifelessly walked towards their broken home. Her eyes filled with tears of regret and sorrow. The signs were always we're always there. She just refused to see them, because he was Noah's dad and she loved him.

The Long Road Ahead

Blinded by love, that cost her everything, Elizabeth found herself broken and her world shattered once again.

Chapter 15

The thick morning fog was clearing, as Elizabeth and Jason argued. It seemed they were doing a lot of that lately. Elizabeth was torn between leaving Jason or trying to make things work. Elizabeth began to grow stronger in her faith and Jason had not changed. And from the looks of things, he was not even trying to. He wanted Elizabeth and Noah, but he didn't want to change his lifestyle. He was continually heading down a road that Elizabeth was not willing to travel. He was still drinking even more and staying out till the early parts of the morning, with his new friends. All Elizabeth could think about was Noah, she wanted a better life for him. Elizabeth wanted Noah to grow up with both his parents in a secure and loving household. That was something she never had. And she wanted it so bad for Noah. But at what cost was she willing to give him that? The phone rang, Jason answered and left the house in a hurry. Elizabeth had gotten to the point that she didn't even ask

The Long Road Ahead

anymore. Jason was in such a rush that he left his coat behind. Before Elizabeth knew it, she found herself searching though Jason's coat pockets. She found a piece of paper with the name and number of a female. Elizabeth tried not to jump to conclusion, but anger took over quickly.

Every horrible thought she could think of flooded her mind. Before she knew it, she was dialing the numbers.

A soft voice on the other line said hello Jason, I was waiting for your call. Elizabeth couldn't believe what she heard, she quickly hung up the phone and screamed at the top of her lungs.

A relentless fire burned inside of her, and she begin to throw anything that was in her way. The house was a mess and thankfully, Noah slept through it all. She waited for Jason to return, with eyes burning with fury. The door opened slowly and Jason came in and they argued all night. Both of them were sleep deprived as the morning arose. They had accomplished nothing, they were no longer two in love, but enemies of love. Elizabeth checked in on Noah and got his breakfast ready, for when he woke. After, she decided to step outside for some fresh air. She was tired, hungry and outraged by the thoughts of Jason being unfaithful, especially after she stayed with him, with all his empty

Chapter 15

promises of changing. LIES! Elizabeth was filled with so much anger! How could she be so foolish. In that anger, she ran back upstairs and grabbed a small sharp utensil and went back downstairs and made her mark on Jason's truck, that he loved so dearly. Elizabeth felt a moment of relief, until she realized what she had just done. Anger only fixes a problem temporary, then we must face the consequences for your actions. Elizabeth was ashamed of what she had done in that moment of weakness.

Shaken up and overwhelmed with anxiety and fear, Elizabeth slowly made her way back to the apartment. Elizabeth wanted to tell Jason of the horrible thing she had just done, but fear of his action terrified her.

Lying on the couch with her head buried in the pillow, trying to figure out how to fix what she had done, the doorbell rang. Elizabeth knew it could not be anything good. It was the neighbor at the door. Elizabeth, felt like she was having a panic attack. She couldn't hear what they were saying, but soon after, Jason left the apartment and headed down stairs. Jason returned yelling and Elizabeth refused to face him. She knew what she had did and now it was out. Elizabeth began to cry, enraged with anger Jason lost his control and slapped her right across the back. Then he grabbed keys his and left the apartment. Elizabeth was shaken by what happen and could not fully process what was. Jason had never hit her before and Elizabeth vowed that day, he never would again. Battered and broken, Elizabeth packed up her car with what she could for her and Noah. She started up the car and sat there for a few minutes, as she looked in the rear-view mirror. Driving away, Elizabeth left behind the betrayal, the abuse and another failed love affair.

"Why do we always choose what's not good for us? Perhaps we think we don't deserve anything better.

"The heart of man plans his way, but the Lord establishes his steps" (Proverbs 16:9). As human beings, we will never stop making plans, but perhaps a lesson for us is to hold our plans lightly.

Jason made his choice and without looking back, Elizabeth made hers.

Not knowing where they were going, she kept driving.

So many emotions flooded Elizabeth's mind as she drove with tears in her eyes. Foolishly always searching for love, she trusted that God would bring her out of her reoccurring nightmare. They were lost and Elizabeth's surroundings were unfamiliar. Noah was hungry and she couldn't stop crying. Elizabeth tried to shake the daunting thoughts

Chapter 15

from her head. Noah was her main priority now. Her world was over and their never seemed to be a good time to mourn her losses. The only thing real in her life was Noah and Elizabeth had to do what was best for him. It was dark and Elizabeth kept driving there was not a store in sight. She had no one to call and only a few dollars. Fear began to take over, she had no control of her life and Noah needed her. She screamed out; "Oh my God, help me please, someone help me and when she looked up, a brightly lighted police station was before her. Elizabeth got Noah out the car and slowly walked inside. She was lost and had nowhere to go. She walked in and froze, as the police office asked "how can I help you, Miss?" Elizabeth felt faint from the heaviness she was carrying physically and mentally.

She fell to the floor and begin to sob with Noah in her arms. The officers helped her off the floor and into the chair. Elizabeth slowly turned to the officer and sobbed as she blurted out "I can't believe he hit me!" The officer helped Elizabeth file a restraining order against Jason, but she didn't want to press charges, she still loved him and he was Noah's dad. Elizabeth tried her best to compose herself, as she filed the report. She told the officers she had no place to go and no one to call.

They were homeless. The officer informed Elizabeth of a nearby women's shelter for battered women

The Long Road Ahead

and their children. She couldn't believe all this was happening, she was a victim of abuse. Elizabeth followed behind the officers, to the women's shelter. When they arrived two tall Caucasian women were waiting at the door. After talking with the officers, the ladies looked over at Elizabeth with warm smiles. They introduced their selves, as Laura and Susan. They were friendly and help Elizabeth with Noah and her things. It was late, Susan showed Elizabeth where she could get a bite to eat and feed Noah. While Noah ate, Laura had Elizabeth look over policies and paperwork and sign. After Noah finished eating, Laura showed them to their room.

Elizabeth washed Noah up and changed his clothes. She tucked him in and softly sang to him, his favorite lullaby and before she knew it he was fast asleep. Elizabeth looked around her strange environment and tears begin to stream down her cheeks. Overwhelmed with emotion, Elizabeth grabbed Noah pulled him close and laid down on the unfamiliar bed in her unfamiliar environment.

Chapter 16

Morning came quickly, Elizabeth was still mentally exhausted and tired from the battles of yesterday. She set up on the side of the bed, trying not to awake Noah. The aroma in the air smelled of breakfast, and Elizabeth was hungry. The knock on the door woke Noah. Elizabeth opened the door, to find a strange, but familiar face.

It was Laura, "will you be joining us for breakfast?'

Elizabeth shook her head yes and picked up Noah and followed her to the dining area. Breakfast was delicious and Noah had a hardy appetite. He hadn't a clue what was going on, but he was happy and that was all that matter. After breakfast was over, Laura waved for Elizabeth to come to her office. They talked and filled out some more forms. The people at the shelter were kind, but Elizabeth stayed to herself. Elizabeth ended up staying at the women's shelter for a month. She made the best

The Long Road Ahead

of each day and seeing Noah playing and smiling made it a little easier at times. Elizabeth worked with Laura and Susan, daily to put a plan of action into motion. Elizabeth only ad 30 days, but every day she worked hard on moving forward.

Although, Thoughts of why it happened, what ifs and why she wasn't enough always seemed to sneak into her thoughts and strangle out the little peace she had.

The next day, everything changed for Elizabeth! Laura and Susan were able to set Elizabeth up with a job, an apartment and child care for Noah. It seemed too good to be true, everything was happening so fast, it was like waking up to a fairy tale. Elizabeth was finally going to have her own place and the very thought of it all scared her to death.

Chapter 17

Elizabeth and Noah were now settling into their new apartment. The first couple of days were rough. Elizabeth was trying to suppress the constant battles on the inside that was trying to surface to the outside.

The frustration of her past didn't make it easy to move forward and the feeling of loneliness kept growing stronger every day. The feeling was constant and Elizabeth didn't know how to be alone. Elizabeth had reconnected with her old friend again and their friendship made dealing with the white noise in her head a little less overwhelming. It was nice to have Grace around, but Elizabeth still felt lost.

Grace was a good friend, but Elizabeth always felt judged by her. Grace always made an effort to somehow make her life look flawless compared to others. There was a lot of things Elizabeth, could talk to her about. Elizabeth was not even sure, that Grace even knew how she made her feel. To try and tell her would always end in an argument.

"Daily rechecks on our attitudes and the way we view things can help us prevent a loss in our relationships."

To Elizabeth, it seemed that Grace was always bragging on how she never gave in to temptation and how she always chose the right paths. Grace had never been in a relationship and she was hardly ever sympathetic with Elizabeth or showed any empathy.

"Sometimes being a good friend means; just listening and learning to react with compassion and love, even if we don't understand".

Elizabeth knew Grace wouldn't understand the fight from within. She just wanted someone to be there and perhaps just listen.

Elizabeth hardly understood it herself. In addition, Grace was struggle trying to survive financially. Meanwhile, because of their encounter, Elizabeth started going to church more. She joined the praise team and tried to stay involved as much as she could. She felt safe there, but as soon as she left to go home, the attacks came on. Reading the bible helped a little. When Elizabeth felt shattered and

Chapter 17

the heartache was unbearable, she always turned to Psalms 51 of the bible.

Elizabeth loved that whole scripture, especially when it got to the part "create in me a clean heart and renew a right spirit within me. Don't cast me from your presence or take your holy spirit from me. Restore in me the joy of your salvation." It felt good to be in God's presence, but for Elizabeth it didn't last long. She was determined, but her life was full of pain and at times life seemed hard to bear. Still Elizabeth always found the strength to pressed forward! She worked hard at her new job and even enrolled herself back into school.

Grace and Elizabeth hang out as much as they could. Jason started coming around, after Elizabeth reached out to him. She needed help and after all he was Noah's father. Elizabeth didn't like it one bit, but it was the right thing to do. After a few weeks, Elizabeth felt more comfortable with him, she allowed Noah visit with Jason on occasions.

Chapter 18

Elizabeth was off on Wednesdays and Grace asked Elizabeth if she could have a ride, she needed to talk to her about something. Elizabeth, was always there for Grace when she needed her. Grace asked to hang out at her place, so they could talk. Grace didn't have a steady paying job and she needed a place to stay. Without giving it a thought Elizabeth blurted out of course! She was excited to help, she could use the company and Grace could help out with Noah. "Roommates" Elizabeth and Grace became roommates, Elizabeth gave Grace Noah's room and Noah moved in with Elizabeth. Elizabeth was happy at first, she hated being alone.

Life was started was having its better days. Although, Elizabeth still felt something was missing. The reoccurring feeling of emptiness always seemed to make its way in. One Sunday morning, Elizabeth just wanted to sleep in. She had no motivation to get out of bed. Noah was up most of the night and

Chapter 18

Elizabeth couldn't sleep with all her thoughts. She could hear Grace getting ready for church. She had no choice but to get moving, she was Grace's ride. So, to keep the peace, Elizabeth mustard up what little strength she had and herself and Noah ready. Elizabeth's head was in the clouds for most of the service, she just couldn't focus. Looking around, she noticed Aaron the guitar player from church. He kept starring at her hard and Elizabeth couldn't stop smiling.

Elizabeth tried not to make contact. It was awkward, but she enjoyed the attention he was putting out. It had been a while since Elizabeth had that kind of attention and she loved it. After church Elizabeth and Grace invited a few friends over to hang out. They dropped Noah off with his dad, then hurried home to clean up and prepare for company. It wasn't long before the doorbell rang, their friends started arriving. Elizabeth ran to the door to greet everyone. It had turned out to be a nice get together. They mingled, ate and laughed. The doorbell rang again. When Elizabeth went to open the door, she was all smiles. It was her friend Chris, but he was not alone. He had bought Aaron. Before she could say anything, Chris said "I hope you don't mind, I brought Aaron along.

Elizabeth took a deep breath smiled, gave Chris a friendly hug and said "of course not" any friend of

The Long Road Ahead

yours is a friend of mine. They proceeded upstairs. Everyone was laughing and having a good time. Aaron tried several times to make contact with Elizabeth, but she did everything she could to stay busy and avoid him. It was getting late and Aaron made his way over to Elizabeth. Elizabeth saw him approaching from the corner of her eyes and she was nervous. She didn't really know much about him; except they went to the same church and he was an amazing guitar player. Elizabeth had never noticed before, but Aaron was quite attractive! He was tall, with chocolate skin and his body physique was well defined. He was a pretty-boy indeed, with a boyish smile and a fire in his eye that called for her.

Aaron finally made his way over to her and they started talking. He was charming and knew the right words to get her going. He made her laugh and their chemistry was strong.

Aaron was a little younger than Elizabeth, they both were in college. They seemed to get along well and had some things in common. It was late and the guest were starting to leave, but Elizabeth was lost in Aaron's charm. Aaron stayed behind and they became more acquainted. Elizabeth knew she should have bid him a good night and farewell, but she could not. She was over taken by the

Chapter 18

attention he was giving. He even helped her and Grace clean up.

Grace was tired and went straight to bed. Aaron stayed a little longer. They watched TV, talked, laughed and got to know one another. Elizabeth tried hard to fight the feeling of sexual attraction between them and the need to be held. Aaron's charm was stronger than her will to fight and before Elizabeth knew it, she was hooked! She found herself wrapped in his muscular arms. He kissed her passionately! Lust had taken her completely over and she lay with him that night. Elizabeth fell for him quickly, but she felt horrible, that was not who she was!

She didn't even really know him, but he held her that night and Elizabeth wanted to be loved.

Chapter 19

Blinded by his charm and sexual attraction, they become a couple and Elizabeth had jumped into another relationship. Elizabeth was all in, as always, she really wanted their relationship to work. Her love and attraction for Aaron grew fast and strong. Grace liked Aaron, just not for Elizabeth. Grace was not good about saying things in love. She repeatedly told Elizabeth how stupid she was, and how Aaron was not good for her. Grace believed he only cared about himself and he only wanted one thing (sex).

Elizabeth knew that Aaron had a selfish way about himself and he enjoyed attention. They were getting to know each other and seeing where fate would take them. Grace's attitude towards their relationship really frustrated Elizabeth. Elizabeth started to believe that Grace didn't want to see her happy. She was always saying something negative when it came to Elizabeth's life. For someone who

Chapter 19

had never been in a relationship Grace had a lot to say. Elizabeth was not blind to Aaron's arrogance. She did realize, that she did the majority of the work in the relationship, but she chose to enjoy it and just be in the moment. She just wanted a little happiness and Aaron was that for her. Elizabeth knew she was compromising her destiny for the temporary solution for all she had been though. But it felt good and so Aaron became her distraction from all the misery she kept bottled up inside.

Elizabeth and Grace's friendship was becoming toxic. Unspoken words and unspoken feelings filled the air. Despite everything between them, Elizabeth agreed to help out Grace's cousins, who had been evicted from their apartment. Grace' s cousins stayed with them until they were able to get on their feet. Three more mouth to feed! Even though Elizabeth was overwhelmed and they were struggling themselves, she was always willing and happy to help out. Elizabeth always had a big heart and love triumphed everything in her world. Elizabeth didn't realize the load she had taken on. Her heart was in it, but she was not prepared physically, mentally and emotionally. With every passing day, she became more stressed and agitated with everything and everyone. Elizabeth was the only one who had a steady job. Grace and her cousins tried their best to help out, but the tasks were endless and privacy was limited.

The Long Road Ahead

Elizabeth was juggling too much on her plate. A household, a child, work, school, bills and a new found relationship. Elizabeth knew it was all too much, but she wasn't one really to ask for help. Failure was not an option, so she kept pressing forward. Aaron didn't come around as much, with all of the new commotion. He became frustrated with the lack of privacy they had, when they were together.

The household bills were piling up with the extra mouths. Grace tried to help out as much as she could, but her job didn't pay well, it was more like volunteering.

The feeling of emptiness and not being enough never failed to sneak into her thoughts and snatch her innocence. The wounds from they were inside were deep and starting to resurface. Elizabeth just couldn't escape her past. She felt like she was losing her mind by the minute.

Chapter 20

Grace and Elizabeth started to grow apart with all the unspoken words and tension in the air. Elizabeth felt alone and taken advantage of by everyone. The voices from within grew stronger and louder. There was a constant battle going on in the inside of her head and she was losing fast. It was then she decided to seek outside help. Elizabeth secretly sought out a psychiatrist, who immediately diagnose her Bipolar- schizophrenia depressive disorder. Elizabeth started taking all sorts of medication and begin to gain weight. Elizabeth worked most days and attending school at night, all while keeping her therapy and meds a secret. To deal with everything, Elizabeth became more dependent on the medication.

She'd rather medicate herself then deal with the pressure of life that weighed her down.

The Long Road Ahead

Elizabeth was silently suffering on the inside. Aaron and her were still together. They had a strange relationship and a different kind of love. He loved her and she loved him and they just live in the moment.

They finally had an evening to themselves. They mostly watched studied and watched TV. Aaron kept staring passionately at Elizabeth! She knew he wanted her, but she had to study for her exam. Elizabeth tried her best not to make eye contact, but the attraction was strong. It made her very uncomfortable. Aaron was acting strange all night, fidgeting in his pockets, as if he was a little boy with a new toy. Elizabeth wanted so badly to entertain Aarons seductive attraction, but she had to pass tomorrow's exam and she kept studying. Finally, Aaron took his hand out of his pocket and set his fists on top of her book. Elizabeth looked up at him and his eyes were filled with passion and he had a boyish smile on his face. She looked down as he opened his fist! A ring! An engagement ring was staring back at her. Elizabeth was so confused about his actions and what was happening. She smiled, as if he was playing a joke on her. And then he said it "Will you marry me"? They loved each other but marriage, Elizabeth thought. Sure, they had their differences, it was just, Aaron never really seemed like he wanted to settled down with her. Elizabeth looked into his eyes, that were singing a love song to her that she couldn't resist.

Aaron placed the ring on her finger. And in that moment, she jumped into his arms and said yes! They passionately sealed the night and went their separate ways.

It was a new day and Elizabeth was engaged. So why didn't she feel Engaged? Shouldn't she be happy, and shouting it from the rooftops? Shouldn't she be planning for the biggest day of her life? Elizabeth or Aaron hadn't told anyone about their engagement. It was all happening so fast and it didn't seem real. Aaron had just pointed out his dream girl a few days before. It made Elizabeth feel small, but that was just how he was. They just had so many differences. Elizabeth really did love him and she couldn't understand why that wasn't enough.

Elizabeth was tired of failure and she really just wanted something in her life to work out. In the days ahead Elizabeth behavior began to change. Out of the blue she was begin taking more medication and making poor life choices. Elizabeth

The Long Road Ahead

began missing work and school just to spend time with Aaron. She continued to go to church mostly, because Aaron was there. Elizabeth was infatuated with Aaron, but she was not sure if she really loved him or if he even really loved her. No one knew about the proposal, and they never really spoke about it afterwards. Elizabeth was happy with Aaron, but she wanted more and she had Noah to think about. The thought of starting over made her feel sick to the stomach, so she continued to stick it out with Aaron. Anything was better than nothing at all.

Chapter 21

One Saturday afternoon, while hanging out at Aarons house, Aaron decided to go and visit a neighborhood acquaintance. The house was in walking distance. It was a nice day, so Elizabeth and Aaron walked there together. Aaron knocked on the door and walked in straight to the back and Elizabeth followed behind him. Aaron began talking and Elizabeth peered around the corner. She looked straight ahead at a browned skinned boy, then turned and looked towards the right and she saw him! In that moment Elizabeth froze and her life had nearly flashed before her. Elizabeth felt as though someone had turned off the gravity. It seemed that time had stopped and they were the only two in the room. Elizabeth's heart and mine were free at that moment. It was like everything made sense, as she envisioned herself with this stranger, running through a field filled with beautiful lilies.

The Long Road Ahead

She saw her life with him filled with many sweet encounters. Elizabeth couldn't explain what she feeling! She knew him! He was the man of her dreams. There was such a connection, from deep within. Elizabeth was lost in the atmosphere of what had taken her over. She had forgotten the world around her. It was as though nothing else mattered and it felt like he was the only real reason for her true existence. She didn't want to leave or lose it; she was happy and fulfilled. Shaken out of her brief daze, which seemed like a lifetime. Elizabeth realized that everyone was staring at her. She glanced once again at her surroundings and quickly blurted out "Wow their identical twins". Everyone laughed as Elizabeth tried to make sense of what just happened. Aaron introduced Elizabeth to the boys. Lance and Larry were their names. Lance was one who took her breath away.

Aaron and Elizabeth stayed only a short while. Elizabeth couldn't say another word, she just stood they as they talked, trying not to stare at Lance. She was puzzled by what she was feeling.

Did she have an out of body experienced? Did she experience love at first sight?

Did she fall deeply in love with a stranger, who she just met? After the short visit Aaron and Elizabeth went back to her apartment hang out for a while.

Chapter 21

Elizabeth was distracted most of the evening. She couldn't stop thinking about him! She could never forget his face. This feeling was all new and confusing all at once, she cared about Aaron. What did all this mean?

Chapter 22

Sunday morning had come quick, Elizabeth over slept and church was in an hour. Jason had just dropped Noah off. Elizabeth felt nausea and drained, but her and Grace made it on time.

Elizabeth was still feeling nausea and she just wanted to sleep. The service seemed longer than usual, but it was fulfilling as always. There was afternoon service and Elizabeth wanted so desperately to go home, but she had committed to singing. The church was feeding dinner, in a few. Elizabeth, couldn't wait, she felt as though she was starving. She had decided to go down to the corner store to get a snack for both, herself and Noah. Elizabeth, Noah and two of her church acquaintance's, headed to the store for some snacks.

The store was only 2 minutes away, but Elizabeth's feet were hurting and she had to carry Noah, so they drove.

Chapter 22

They picked up some snacks and headed back to church. Elizabeth stopped to make a left turn into the church parking lot. As, she waited for the cars to pass, out of nowhere a big gray truck speeding and distracted, didn't realize Elizabeth was stopped and slammed right in the back of her car. The impact was hard and Elizabeth black out for only a few seconds. In shock and shaking, she looked over and her Pastor was standing over her. "Elizabeth, she said "it's okay, you were in an accident, I need you to calm down for me." Elizabeth looked at her surroundings and anxiety took over. The ambulance arrived and assessed Elizabeth and the others. The paramedics stabilized Elizabeth in a neck brace and only her and Noah were taken to the hospital.

The ride to the hospital only increased Elizabeth's anxiety. The paramedics had to give Elizabeth something for pain and something to calm her down. When they arrived, Elizabeth was calm but woke. She was confused on her whereabouts and she felt an unbelievable urge to use the bathroom. She looked over a saw Grace and her mother Pearl, with were standing beside her. Elizabeth was relieved to see Noah in his mom-mom's arms. How do you feel baby, said Elizabeth's mom?" Elizabeth grabbed her stomach and said "I really have to go to the bathroom. The pressure was unbearable, Grace went to go get the nurse. Elizabeth had been given a sedative medicine for pain, so the nurse brought her a bedpan, but Elizabeth refused it.

Elizabeth just knew she was constipated and needed to move her bowels. She insisted on going to the bathroom. The nurse assisted Elizabeth to the bathroom and told her she would wait for her outside. Elizabeth was relieved as she sat on the toilet, the pain hit again and she barred down. The pressure was intense and Elizabeth continued to push and a finally the release had come.

Elizabeth felt strange and extremely exhausted unaware of what had just occurred. She felt even weaker than before. She just sat there and rested. Then she heard a knock on the door. "Are you okay?" "Just finishing up" Elizabeth replied. Elizabeth mustarded up the strength to stand up and slowly turn around to flush. She couldn't believe what she was looking at. It was a fetus! Elizabeth was pregnant and the pain she was experiencing was a spontaneous abortion.

Elizabeth was pregnant and had no clue of the pregnancy until now. Shocked and confused, Elizabeth rubbed her eyes and begin to panic, anxiety struck. Without another thought, she reacted to the devastating trauma that had just occurred. Elizabeth grabbed the handle and flushed what seemed to be her fetus. It all happened so fast, Elizabeth stood

Chapter 22

there numb and in disbelief. Tears started to fall as she washed her hands. Elizabeth wiped her tears and something in her changed in that moment. She put the thought of what happened out of her mind and her mind went to a place of safety. She opened the door and the nurse helped her, as she walked lifelessly back to her bed. Let us know if you need anything else, the nurse said as she helped Elizabeth back into bed. Elizabeth curled up into the fetus position, closed her eyes tightly, as they filled with tears and drifted off to sleep.

Chapter 23

Hours later Elizabeth was awakened by the nurse to prepare her for discharge, Elizabeth mom Pearl had taken her and Noah home. Grace was there when they arrived and she help Elizabeth into bed. Still in denial of what took place in the bathroom at the hospital, Elizabeth said not a word to anyone. Saying it out loud would make it a reality and she was not willing or able to face this one.

Grace watched Noah that night so Elizabeth could sleep. The next morning, Pearl came to check on Elizabeth and took Noah, so Elizabeth could take it easy. Elizabeth was in a lot of pain mentally and physically from the accident and was left with no transportation. Elizabeth had been excused from work for a few weeks and she did nothing but sit on the couch, eat and sleep. The feeling of despair, regret and shame weighed heavily on her heart, mind.

Chapter 23

Grace took another job babysitting, which took up most of her time. Elizabeth was alone for most of her recovery. The accident had left her with no transportation. Noah was with his dad and she missed him dearly.

Elizabeth began taken her meds more and eating to ease the pain, the numbness and the racing thoughts. She had not seen or heard from Aaron for a couple of days and Elizabeth didn't care one bit, she felt like he abandoned her.

One evening as Elizabeth curled up on the couch watching tv, the doorbell rang. She was surprised when she opened the door, it was Aaron. She let him in without a word said. He followed her to the living room. They talked for a while. Aaron did most of the talking, and it was mostly about him. He never said one word about the accident. Elizabeth world was broken and Aaron's self-centeredness begin to annoy her, as she tried her hardest to be civil.

All he could about was school and others things that didn't matter. Aaron made comments about her being lazy and gaining weight. Elizabeth had, had enough and they started arguing. She yelled at him for being absent and not coming to the hospital to see about her. Elizabeth didn't want to argue, so she asked him to leave. Aaron headed for the

The Long Road Ahead

stairs, Elizabeth noticed he forgot his phone, so she threw it at him along with the ring he had given her. Aaron picked up the ring and the scattered pieces of his phone and slammed the door and never returned. Aaron and Elizabeth were over...

Chapter 24

Elizabeth found herself secluded from her family and friends once again. The pain and despair of life had caught up with her and she found herself yet in another prison of life. The events of her past and present became overwhelming and Elizabeth was admitted to the psychiatric ward. She had given up on life and didn't care if she lived or died. Elizabeth still never spoke about the traumatic dramatic event that occurred in the hospital. She spent two weeks in the psychiatric ward. There, she rested, taking different kinds of medications, seeing and talking with different doctors and going to group therapy. The only visitor she had was her Pastor. Elizabeth followed the rules, all while trying to cope with her broken inner self. At the end of the two weeks, the doctors cleared Elizabeth to go home, but the emptiness was still there. Grace had kept up the apartment while Elizabeth was gone. Jason was taking care of Noah and had no ideal of

The Long Road Ahead

Elizabeth where abouts. She asked him to watch Noah while she went out of town for a month.

Elizabeth took an extra few days before she informed Jason she was back in town.

Elizabeth knew she had to pull herself together before getting Noah back. She tried going back to church, but it was too hard seeing Aaron. She still cared for him, but he was not good for her. There was too much damaging history, secrets and unspoken words. In addition to Aaron, her life was still turned upside down, she was alone, her and bills were behind. Elizabeth had lost her job, she missed to many days and she was behind in school. She had some income from the accident. It was enough to catch up on some bills and maybe get her through a couple of months. Elizabeth had to get her life in order, before she made any attempt to call for Noah.

For the next month, Elizabeth focused her attention more on trying to get a job and finishing up she's up her college semester. It was hard looking for a job with everything that was going on and having no transportation didn't help, but Elizabeth managed. Elizabeth was determined to try and keep things together.

Early the next morning, Elizabeth received a call from the medical center, she had applied for. They

Chapter 24

wanted to know if she had time to an he had time to interview today or tomorrow. Elizabeth didn't have transportation, but she was excited and hopeful. She scheduled the interview for that day. She missed Noah dearly and this was the first step to getting him back into her arms. She prepared herself and her mind for the scheduled interview and arrived early. Elizabeth nailed the interview and she was hired on the spot! She was set to start her new job, in a week. Elizabeth had a job! Now all she needed was a car. Elizabeth looked daily through the papers, but everything was so expensive or needed repairs. Elizabeth was ready to give up, when she came across a car, with a fair price and in good running condition. It had minor interior issues, but nothing serious.

She called the number to see if she could check the car out and possibly purchase it. The person on the other end said, "sure can you come later this evening?" Elizabeth let out a joyful yes! Elizabeth explained that she did not have transportation. So, the man on the other line, agreed to meet her at the parking lot near her house, which was in walking distance for her.

Elizabeth went to look at the car in a vacant lot and the man she was to meet was Aaron father. Elizabeth was shocked to see it was him, but he hugged her and said he was glad it was her. Aaron

The Long Road Ahead

dad, always like Elizabeth and her personality. They talked and discussed the car. The car was 2,500, that was all of Elizabeth's savings. She had no choice they needed transportation. Elizabeth gave him the money and he gave her back $1000. Elizabeth smiled, her eyes filled with tears, as she gave him a big hug of thanks. Favor was on her side, God always made away for her. Elizabeth was on the road again and life was starting to fall into place.

Chapter 25

Grace had got a new job, that required her to move and with everything that Elizabeth and Grace had been though space was truly what they both needed. They kept in contact as much as their busy schedules would allow.

Elizabeth always had fear of being alone, she suffered a lot from feeling unloved, loneliness and the reoccurring feeling of emptiness. Elizabeth tried to develop a closer relationship with the Lord, by reading her Bible more, praying daily and trying to go to church more. The distraction of Aaron, work, school, Noah and keeping a roof over their heads was extremely draining and overwhelming. It seemed like the more she tried the harder life got. Jason helped out with Noah as much as he could, but Elizabeth did everything in her power to not rely on anyone for help. Jason and Elizabeth were not in a great place, especially after the custody battle and child support orders. Elizabeth tried

The Long Road Ahead

dating other people again and kept falling into the same prison of searching for love in all the wrong places. "We accept the love we think we deserve. When it's not really love, but in addiction to mask the real pain".

After a few failed relationships, Elizabeth made up in her mind that she was giving up on love. There was a wall around her heart and she believed that love was just not in the cards for her. Elizabeth was discouraged traveling down the same road of unhappiness. Her prayer was; she just wanted someone to love her unconditionally for who she was and someone who really saw her.

Clearly the path she was taking seemed to only lead to heart break and disappointment.

In the days ahead, Elizabeth tried her best to put all her energy and time into Noah, herself and trying to moving forward. She worked hard physically and mentally trying to survive as a single mother. She did her best to stay focused, but no matter how hard she tried, the rewind button of her past always seemed to resurrect itself. It seemed the more she pushed forward, the harder it got.

Chapter 26

Elizabeth was determined to keep moving forward. She worked and studied hard and put all her attention into raising Noah, but it was not enough.

One evening at work, Elizabeth was asked to stay over, because someone had called out sick. Elizabeth was tired, but she needed the extra money and it was only for a few hours. She called Jason, to see if he could keep Noah and take him to pre- school in the morning. Jason agreed, but not before letting Elizabeth know how he felt. He was a good dad, but Jason always gave Elizabeth a hard time when she needed extra help. The evening was slowly moving along. Elizabeth's supervisor, asked her to go down to the first floor, to the get supplies for the rooms. Elizabeth took her time getting to her destination, instead of taking the elevator she took the stairs. The door was locked

The Long Road Ahead

when she arrived to the supply room so, she rang the bell for assistance.

The door opened slowly and Elizabeth heart dropped to her feet, it was him, the man she met. It was Lance.

She couldn't talk or move; her heart was pounding as if it was trying to break out of her chest.

After just starring at one another, Lance said "is there something I can help you with?" She couldn't understand why her mouth couldn't do what her mind wanted. Elizabeth brain was foggy, she was lost for words, embarrassed she handed him the list of supplies, she needed. On Elizabeth way back to her unit, Elizabeth was all smiles, she couldn't help thinking that this had to be fate. What was the odds of getting a great job and meeting the man of her dreams all in the same week?

Work seemed even better than before and Elizabeth was on a mission to find out what was next. Elizabeth asked one of her work associates, if they knew anything about the guy who worked downstairs. Ben happened to be good friends with Lance. From that day forward Elizabeth made extra efforts to run into Lance, he seemed liked her and he enjoyed her frequent visits. They became closer everyday talking laughing. Work buddies? Elizabeth decided to test whatever it was that they had. She asked

Chapter 26

Lance if he was dating anyone? His reply was no, he had just gotten out of a serios relationship and was not looking to get into another one. Elizabeth was crushed by those words, but given up was not an option. Fate had got her this far and she was not about give in now. Elizabeth started hanging out more with Ben, to get to know more about Lance. Ben and Elizabeth hang out almost every day. Until, Ben began to think Elizabeth was interested in him. After work Ben walked Elizabeth to her car and leaned in to kiss her.

She pulled back and explained to him that she liked him, but just as a friend.

This was all a misunderstanding and she told him that she was interested in Lance. After that encounter, seeing Ben became awkward for Elizabeth. She felt bad about the whole misunderstanding, he was truly a good work friend.

Chapter 27

Elizabeth learned Lance worked on computers and she used that information to her advantage. The next time Elizabeth ran into Lance, Elizabeth explained to him that she was having some problems with her computer. Lance told her that he could take a look at it, later after work, if she wanted him to.

Elizabeth was excited, but tried to keep calm as they exchanged numbers and Elizabeth gave him her address. Elizabeth left early that day from work, which gave her time to go home and tidy up. Lance would soon be over and Elizabeth had no clue had to explain to him what was wrong with her computer. It was brand new, not even a month old. There was nothing physically wrong with it. Lance had pulled up and Elizabeth panicked, without thinking pulled out every cord she could see. The doorbell rang and Elizabeth hurried to bring herself together, she opened the door and there he

Chapter 27

was just like he promised. Elizabeth led him to her computer room, hoping he would not realize what she had did. Lance got straight to work, it took him less than 15 mins to fix the mess, she had purposely caused. Elizabeth thought it would take longer and she didn't want him to go, so she offered him some juice and invited him to stay and watch a movie with her. Lance was easy going and that night they talked and got to know each a little better. They found closeness in one another and every night from that day forward, they begin a wonderful and fulfilling friendship. Elizabeth and Lance had been seeing one another for six months, they really cared deeply for one another, but no one spoke of it.

They were friends who enjoyed one another's company, never speaking or acting on of the strong attraction they had for each other. Being friends was okay, it was great, but it felt like more than just friends to Elizabeth.

Chapter 28

They spent Valentine Day spent together watching movies and laughing, Elizabeth turned to Jamal and asked "what are we doing? Are we just friends or are we sort of dating? Lance looked over at Elizabeth and their eyes met as he said I guess were dating. Elizabeth chuckled and held hands and starred at one another. The cat was out of the bag and the burning passion that they tried so hard to hold back started to burst from the seams. Elizabeth made the first move, she moved closer and said to him "am so sorry but I've been waiting to do this for a long time". Elizabeth climbed on to Lance's lap and kissed his lips passionately.

Lance passionately kissed her back, then gently picked Elizabeth up never breaking the seal of their first kiss and headed towards her room. Lance slowly placed Elizabeth down and asked her if she was sure, Elizabeth shook her head and they had

Chapter 28

their first passionate encounter. Elizabeth eyes begin to fill with tears, it was like it was her first time ever being touched. He was the perfect verse in her love song. He made her feel as though, she was customed designed just for him.

Lance was amazing inside and out, he was everything she wanted and more, Elizabeth didn't want the night to end. Lance stayed as long as he could, but had to go home but not before reassuring Elizabeth he would see her tomorrow. Elizabeth was memorized by the magical night that had had taken place and looked forward to the new journey ahead with Lance...

Chapter 29

Elizabeth was injured at the job and was out for a while, there was not enough income to sustain the incoming bills. Lance and Elizabeth relationship were getting stronger and more serious. They were in love, but she could not bear telling him she was struggling. Elizabeth was stubborn when it came to asking for help or taking handouts. All her life if she had a problem, she fixed it and never asked for help. This time was different though she tried her best a few months later ended up losing everything. Noah and Elizabeth were homeless, they moved in with Terrance a mutual friend of hers and Grace. Terrance had an efficacy apartment with no room to spare, but it was better than nothing, so they made it work.

Lance was still unaware of Elizabeth's circumstances; all he knew was she needed help with Noah and had to concentrate more on her studies.

Chapter 29

Lance knew Elizabeth had a son, but he never met him. Lance never questioned any of Elizabeth's motives and was always there for her when she needed him. After a few weeks Elizabeth lost her job at the medical center, but found a closer job at doctor's office nearby. It was not a job she was fond of, but it helped out and she didn't want to over stay her welcome. Terrance and Elizabeth started to become irritated with one another, with being in such close quarters and the lack of privacy. Terrance was not use to having a roommate, especially one with a young child.

The only place to have time for yourself was in the bathroom, everything else was an opened space.

Elizabeth tried all she could to stay out of his way and give him space. Terrance work in the evening, so Elizabeth tried to stay out and about on her days off, until she knew he would be ready to leave for work. Elizabeth worked hard to save up so Noah and her could have their own space, but to get an apartment you have to be on your current job for at 6 months to a year. Jason was coming around and took Noah when he could. Elizabeth's never exposed her struggles. Elizabeth needed Jason more than he was willing to be available. They argued a lot, because Jason had no job and always made it a big issue, when she called him to watch Noah.

The Long Road Ahead

Lance always made Elizabeth smile not even knowing how broken she was inside. He was always full of surprises. One evening Lance had invited Elizabeth over to his house for dinner. He had gone out of his way to create a magical evening, he made dinner. They ate and laughed; the food was delicious and the evening was amazing! They crawled up on the couch and watched a movie and Elizabeth fell asleep in his arms. It was getting late and Lance awoke her with a kiss on the forehead. They said their goodbyes and Elizabeth drove back to the apartment. Elizabeth stomach was upset and she went to the bathroom. She washed her face with cold water and the doorbell rang.

She thought Terrance was home early and forgot his key. When she opened the door, on the other side stood Aaron.

Elizabeth was puzzled why he was there and how he found her. She let him in and they talked. Aaron wanted Elizabeth, he wanted to take her in his arms and show her he missed her and apart of her still wanted him. They had one night till dawn, but Elizabeth chose Lance. Elizabeth explained to Aaron how she felt about Lance and she walked him to the door. Aaron hugged her closely and tried to kiss her. Elizabeth turned her head. She knew he felt the little piece of her that wanted him. She loved Aaron, but she was completely in love with

Chapter 29

Lance. Aaron and Elizabeth did have a past, but that past was irreverent to what was transpiring with Lance. Elizabeth softly pushed him out the door and said goodbye, as she closed the door.

Chapter 30

Elizabeth dreaded the bright sun from the morning, she felt miserable, but got ready for work unable to eat or drink. Work seemed extremely long that particular day. Elizabeth could not wait for her break, felt dizzy and light headed all day. She was hungry and they had one more case to go and Elizabeth tried to hang in there, but before she knew it everything went dark and Elizabeth passed out cold on the cold hard floor. Elizabeth woke up confused and in fear of why she was on the ground. The ambulance was called and Elizabeth was in the hospital yet again.

The ER doctor confirmed that Elizabeth was 8 weeks pregnant and extremely dehydrated. They gave her fluids by IV, then discharge her within a few hours.

Pregnant? Elizabeth was afraid of the unknown but another part of her was excited, she just knew

Chapter 30

it was a girl. Lance was working and had no clue of what was taking place, so Elizabeth drove to Terrance's to share the news with him. Terrance was happy for her, but he wanted to know her plans of getting her own place. There was definitely no room for a baby. And he didn't want there to be talk and people assume it's his. It was a while before Elizabeth told Lance, she didn't want to lose him, she loved him so much and they were so great together. She worked hard and went to school, but she couldn't bare keeping this secrete from Lance, he was her best friend, soulmate and lover. He was hers completely and she was his. Nothing else mattered in the world when they were together.

Elizabeth a met Lance at his job for lunch, without a word she handed him the results. Lance looked at her and smiled, gave her a hug and said okay "I will see you after work". Elizabeth was beginning to show a little and Terrance and her had a long conversation concerning their living arrangements. Elizabeth understood Terrance point of view. Terrance and Elizabeth friendship got complicated after they almost engaged and comforted each other in one of Elizabeth's a moment of weakness, in the beginning. They never talked about; they knew what it was and that was that. Elizabeth understood his concerns and with no hard feelings, she started to look for her and Noah a place to call home. With no luck Elizabeth swallowed

The Long Road Ahead

her pride went to her mother, who had remarried and asked to stay there for a while. Living with Elizabeth mother and her new husband was very uncomfortable and Elizabeth tried to stay out of their way. Elizabeth's mom had no idea she was pregnant and Elizabeth tried her hardest to keep it that way. Elizabeth mother showed no interest of wanting Elizabeth there. The stress of being under her mothers' roof again and feeling unwanted, was too much to handle. Elizabeth felt like a child who had no say in what she could and couldn't do. Elizabeth had to make the hardest decision of her life, Elizabeth called Jason and informed him that she had to do her another internship for school and needed him to take care of Noah for a few weeks. Elizabeth said her good byes to Noah and thanked Jason for helping her out.

She drove to the park, parked her car and cried she was homeless once again, with nowhere to go. Lance was still living with his parents, so she didn't want to burden him with her problems. Elizabeth continued t to go to class that evening knowing she had nowhere to lay her head. Her mind was all over the place, when class was over Elizabeth got in her car loaded with her entire life and drove back to the park, parked, cried and fell asleep. For days Elizabeth worked, went to class and maintained her relationship with Lance, all while living in her car.

Chapter 31

Lance was clueless of what was happening right underneath his nose, because Elizabeth always made an effort to meet him where he was.

Elizabeth would sneak over Terrance to shower, eat and relax when she knew he was at work. The nights begin to get colder and Elizabeth had to think for her precious gift growing inside of her. Elizabeth had no choice but to go to the local shelter, it was nice to take a long hot shower without rushing and sleep in a warm bed. The shelters policy was thirty days and there was a curfew unless you had a job that requires you to be out later. Elizabeth continued on seeing Lance while telling him nothing of what was happening, she was to embarrassed and had too much pride to admit defeat. Elizabeth was disappointed in herself and ashamed of her circumstances and the stress of it all was starting to take a toll on the baby. Lance moved out of his parents' house and got a place with his brother Larry

The Long Road Ahead

and his friend Ben. Elizabeth spent most of her days hanging out there, she was homeless, going to school and trying to find a new job, all while trying to hide her reality from Lance.

Elizabeth missed Noah and she worked hard on trying to get them a place to call home, but it was harder than ever and defeat and despair were overriding determination. Elizabeth was still seeing a psychiatrist on and off and never seeing any change. Elizabeth felt her days getting darker and longer, as the scream from inside were pressing to the surface. Elizabeth felt like therapy was just patching up the obvious leaks, and the root of the pressure was growing deeper with each day. She needed help, but asking for help was not one of Elizabeth's strong suits.

Chapter 32

Elizabeth loved Lance dearly, but the thoughts of past relationships haunt her. It seemed her relationship always started off like shooting stars, she waited for something amazing, it was bright, excited and wonderful and in the glimpse of an eye it was gone. Elizabeth seemed to always want to sabotage anything good in her life before it exploded to pieces. Lance was different; with him, she had trouble understanding why her heart wouldn't do what her mind wanted it to. Fate always stepped in when it came to Lance and Elizabeth. Lance started to become more concerned of why Elizabeth never stayed the night, after he got his own place. He wouldn't let it go and finally, he asked Elizabeth why she never wanted to stay with him and why she never invited him over again. Lance wanted to know if they were okay or if someone else had stepped into the picture. Elizabeth really loved Lance and hated keeping this secret from him. There was a long unbreakable pause and stare, as

The Long Road Ahead

she looked at him in despair and broke down and explained everything to him. Lance was a little shocked and a little upset because Elizabeth kept all this from him. But he never harbored over anything, he understood and offer her to stay with him. Elizabeth and Lance had a history of friendship and she realized she didn't have to pretend him and he never did with her.

Chapter 33

Elizabeth went back to the shelter that night and ponder over if moving in with Lance this was a wise choice.

She loved him and there was no doubt in her mind that he loved her back. In the back of her head couldn't help but wonder, if he only wanted her to stay with him because she was carrying his child. She really did manage to fall crazy in love with him, but she wondered if they had enough of what it took to make it last. They were young and still trying to figure out life itself. On the other hand, it would not just be them, but his brother and good friend, as well. The next morning Elizabeth had made decision, she chose to take Lance up on his offer. Elizabeth enjoyed living with Lance it was fun and exciting and he was easy going. Elizabeth and Lance got closer and became serious, they were so in love playing house together. She wanted Lance to meet one of the most important people

The Long Road Ahead

in her life; Noah. Elizabeth talked to Jason and told him she was in town for the weekend and wanted to spend it with Noah, Jason agreed. Lance and Noah's first encounter were good, but a little strange. Lance dint know how response to his presence. Lance to knew Elizabeth had a child, she always talked about him and he was finally there. Noah was the sunshine of her life and full of love and always made the best of his world. Lance loved Elizabeth and Noah was a part of her life and so Lance learned to love Noah as well.

Chapter 34

Elizabeth was happy, everyone she truly loved was under one roof. Life was still a little messy but she was still happily in love. Elizabeth but the reality of it all, was she had a child with one on the way and no sense of stability. Lance and Elizabeth had been together now for three years and Lance was dragging his feet to commit. Elizabeth didn't want to pressure him, but she needed to know where all this playing house was going. She was sick at the fact that Lance was afraid to commit. What more did he need to figure out, they were inseparably in love. Wanting commitment bought a little strain on their relationship. When you think things can't get any worst, they do. Ben decided meet a girl and they became serious and , he ended up moving out. Lance and his brother Larry tried their best to handle the rent, it became too much for them to handle on their own. It was then they made the decision to moved back in with their parents. Elizabeth was devastated she had no job, no

The Long Road Ahead

place to go once again. It was like her story was written and then erased back to the beginning. Elizabeth couldn't catch a break. Elizabeth had no choice but to see if she could get her spot back at the shelter.

Chapter 35

Elizabeth fell into depression again, she wanted Noah to be with her. Lance and Elizabeth continued seeing each other. Commitment was still a big elephant in the room when they were together. They mostly fought and the day it was like it never happen. She was his sweetheart and he was her perfect love song. In the end Lance convinced Elizabeth to come live with him. Lance informed Elizabeth that he had spoken to his parents about their situation and the pregnancy. Elizabeth knew Lance was only trying to do what best for her and the baby, so she agreed. Elizabeth put all her and Noah's things in a storage. The first couple of days living at Lance parents' home, were okay. Elizabeth had meet Lances parents on several occasions. Walter and Vanessa were good people, but Elizabeth's self of esteem plummeted with every waking day. The shame of being pregnant, with no job and living in her boyfriend's parents' basement became a reality that only made things worst.

The Long Road Ahead

Lance reassured Elizabeth that everything would be okay. Elizabeth was so uncomfortable in her current living situation; she had no job and Lance was at work most of the day and left her alone. Lance grandma Ms. Sarah would come over daily to look after the house. Ms. Sarah did not care for Elizabeth and the fact that she was pregnant her grandson child.

She made Elizabeth life miserable every chance she could get. Ms. Sarah didn't believe that Elizabeth was carrying Lance's baby. She started spreading rumors and telling lies of Elizabeth whereabouts and who she really was. Elizabeth tried her best to stay out of her way but it was not easy, she was everywhere. Elizabeth, was thankful though everything she always had a vehicle.

She left the house daily, to try and better herself and to stay away for all the chaos. Elizabeth was not eating right or drinking enough, she just tried to stay out of everyone's way. Elizabeth did not have a job and did not want to eat and drink up their food, if she could not contribute to the household. Elizabeth would not eat until Lance got home. He would always bring her a meal from Bojangles.

Days were long and Elizabeth long to have Noah by her side, but refused to bring him into the living catastrophe she endured. Elizabeth felt like an

Chapter 35

outsider and the walls were caving in on her and she so desperately wanted out.

Lance tired his best to keep her happy, but the truth was Elizabeth was not happy. She didn't want Lance to worry. French fries, nuggets and a vanilla milkshake became her escape and she looked forward to that little taste of peace every night...

Chapter 36

Nine months pregnant Elizabeth still resided with Lance in his parent's basement. The afternoon was quiet and Mrs. Vanessa was off from work that day and Ms. Sarah didn't come over that day. Elizabeth started having contraction and tried her best to tolerate them. Elizabeth helped, Mrs. Vanessa out around the house for aa little while. Elizabeth couldn't not take the pain any longer, she called the doctor and went in to be seen.

Elizabeth was only dilated a couple centimeters and was sent back home. Elizabeth was exhausted for some reason, so she asked Mrs. Vanessa if she needed any help with dinner. Elizabeth helped prepare dinner and when they were done, she went downstairs to take a well needed nap. Elizabeth slept for about a good two hours or so and took a nap and woke up to the worst cramps known to man. Mrs. Vanessa heard her screech from upstairs and came down to find Elizabeth bent over in

Chapter 36

excruciating pain. Mrs. Vanessa, helped Elizabeth up the stairs and drove her straight to the hospital. Lance met them there. Elizabeth wanted her mother, so Mrs. Vanessa called Ms. Pearl and she met them there as well. Elizabeth was definitely in labor, Lance stayed close by her side.

He was so playful, calm and loving that day, but it annoyed Elizabeth to the fullest. The contractions were strong but nothing was happening. The doctor checked Elizabeth and said "we are almost there." They nurse suggested that Elizabeth get up and walk around a little. So, Elizabeth and Jamal walked around the unit. Elizabeth only walked a few steps, until she couldn't take it anymore.

They headed back to the room and Elizabeth was in tears. Elizabeth mom, Pearl helped her into bed and rubbed her back, but nothing was helping. Mrs. Vanessa suggested that Elizabeth get an epidural. Elizabeth had Noah natural and she wanted the same for this baby. The doctor came in and checked Elizabeth once more. Keep moving she's coming, "I'll be back in a few hours", said the doctor. Elizabeth thought for sure it was time and hearing those words "a few hours", she decided to give in to the epidural. They waited while the order was place and after an hour the epidural was placed. The epidural slowed down the birthing process and everyone was getting tired. Elizabeth's mother was

The Long Road Ahead

exhausted, she had worked the nightshift and half of the morning shift. She told Elizabeth she would be back, she just needed to close her eyes for a few. Lance and his mother stayed and slept on the fold out bed. The new baby was stubborn and Elizabeth was in labor all that night.

Chapter 37

The next morning, Elizabeth gave a gentle pushed with every contraction and felt everything. Elizabeth informed the nurse she needed to go to the bathroom.

They wouldn't let her get up because she had the epidural. Elizabeth kept insisting it was not effective and she could walk. Elizabeth continually refused to use the bedpan, the nurse finally gave in and called for help to take Elizabeth to the restroom. With a little struggle she made it to the bathroom. When Elizabeth return from the bathroom, the doctor came shortly after. The doctor checked Elizabeth and called for the nurses; the time had finally come and it was time for the new baby's arrival. After a few successful pushes, she was here.

She was beautiful and finally here! She came into this world on the same day her dad and mom

The Long Road Ahead

officially met. With everything that had transpired between Lance and Elizabeth, they never picked a name. And boy didn't they have trouble agreeing on one. Time was passing their baby was nameless. They were watching a movie on Tv and they both looked up at each and agreed on Lily. Lily was a perfect named for a perfect princess. Jason's mother brought Noah to the hospital to see his new baby sister Lily. Noah loved Lily they bonded right away and he never wanted to leave her side. Elizabeth mom finally made it back to the hospital and held Lily for the first time. Everything was perfect for that moment.

Chapter 38

After a couple of days Lance and Elizabeth took their baby girl home with Noah and started their journey as a family. Expect going back to Lance parent's basement was not a life at all. Life become much harder with all the changes and arrangement. Elizabeth tried her best to cope, but it was all too much. Elizabeth had a melt down when Lance arrived home from work. She wanted to know if what they had was real/ and did he truly love her? And if so, why were they still living in his parent's basement, with a newborn and unmarried? Elizabeth was overwhelmed they talked, and she yelled, until she just gave up. Elizabeth turned away from Lance and cried uncontrollably trying to figure out how and why she ended up here.

Maybe she was experiencing postpartum depression or maybe she was just fed up with where her choices in life landed her. Elizabeth self-worth always got in the way, when it came to love. She loved Lance, he was not the greatest thing in her world, he was her world, but she couldn't live like this anymore. Elizabeth wanted more and she wanted Noah with her. Elizabeth got up and begin packing her belongings. Lance was speechless and sat quietly, as he stated to realize that nothing mattered unless they shared it together. In that moment, Lance grabbed Elizabeth's hand and turned her around to face him. He wiped her tears, kissed her softly and said, "I love you, Elizabeth; will you marry me." Elizabeth looked at him and laughed at the thought of what happened and how this proposal came to be. She couldn't answer him, she wanted it to be real, but the thoughts of him proposing out of obligation filled her mind. Lance knew Elizabeth had been hurt many times and he could see the confusion in her eyes. Elizabeth looked over at Lily and dropped her head, she wanted to say yes. Lance picked up her head and pulled her close to him, as he spoke softly the words, that filled Elizabeth with reassurance. He looked into her eyes and told her he was serious and how before she had come into his life there was no purpose and now the thought of losing her, made him feel an emptiness. He ended, with I always wanted you, I prayed for you and you are here and I love you and letting go was not an option. Elizabeth could not help herself she loved him too with every breath in her body, they kissed and Elizabeth said yes. That night for the first time in months Elizabeth felt happiness that she held

Chapter 38

on to dearly. That same night, Elizabeth threw a couple of random dates into a bowl and that was how they ended up with the perfect wedding date.

Chapter 39

From that date they choose together, they only had six months to plan. Elizabeth was excited she was finally going to be married. They were in love and moving forward. Elizabeth was happy, she was marrying the man of her dreams and nothing else matter. Elizabeth kept herself busy trying to look for a wedding dress, plan a wedding and trying to find a home for her family. Lance and Elizabeth were so caught up in the moment they forgot to tell Lance's parents. They did not get the reaction they expected. Lance's parents sort of brushed it off, like it was just talk. It was not until Elizabeth brought home her wedding dress and they realized that Lance and Elizabeth were serious. Elizabeth didn't let their attitude towards the wedding bother her, she was on a mission and the wedding date was approaching fast. After reality set in with parents, Mrs. Vanessa tried to help out, but it seemed more like she was taken over. Elizabeth just wanted small ceremony and she sought out the help of

Chapter 39

her good friend May, an older lady, she met from church. Elizabeth wanted a small wedding in the chapel with just family, but Lance mother Vanessa, wouldn't have it, she wanted more and Elizabeth just gave in and stepped out of her way. Elizabeth didn't care anymore just as long as Lance and her were married. Elizabeth wanted her mother to be a part of the wedding planning as well, so when the went to look at flowers, she asked her mother Pearl to come. It was a stressful day trying to make everyone happy. When the day was over Elizabeth found strength in the arms of Lance.

Chapter 40

Everything on Elizabeth's end was coming together. Lance started going to church with Elizabeth and they also started marriage counseling. Lance even decided to get baptized. Elizabeth wanted everything to be simple, but perfect and Lance just wanted Elizabeth to be happy.

Lily was six months and getting bigger every day. Ms. Sarah loved her Lily, but despised Elizabeth and refused to be a part of their wedding. Elizabeth was still not Ms. Sarah's favorite person, but every now and then they had a connection, that made Elizabeth smile.

The big Day had finally come, Elizabeth had stayed with her mother Pearl that night. May came over to do Elizabeth make-up and left soon after. While everyone was getting dressed, Elizabeth stepped outside for a brief moment. The day was perfect and the crisp breeze of the air was soothing.

Chapter 40

Elizabeth closed her eyes just for a second and when she opened them, she started walking. Was this what they call cold feet. Elizabeth stopped and looked around and realized, that this was silly and made her way back to her mom's house. They car had come to take the bridal party to the wedding. Elizabeth became a bit nervous, as they arrived. It was like walking into a surprise wedding, she had no clue of what and who to expect. Like all wedding nothing seemed to go right and Elizabeth begin to experience a brief panic attack. Grace was Elizabeth matron of honor and she tried her best to keep Elizabeth calm. It was all too much and overwhelming as Elizabeth stood in front of the fan trying to cool down. Elizabeth remembers not everyone can marry there one true love, but she was about to. Just then May came in and it was time. The doors opened and Elizabeth looked up and their eyes met and everything became much clearer. She walked slowly into her season, to begin the journey with the love of her life.

Chapter 41

Lance and Elizabeth were finally married and after the honeymoon reality kicked in fast. They still were living in the basement of Lance's parents' house with two kids. Elizabeth kept herself busy in search for a home of their own, they had looked a couple of houses but had no luck. Elizabeth was becoming discouraged, but she was determined to have a place where they could be a family. Sunday after church, Elizabeth prayed for a miracle and the Sunday paper gave her just that. Elizabeth saw a 3 bedroom/2-bathroom ranch home for sale. The price was out of their range, but Elizabeth made the appointment to view the home anyway. Elizabeth couldn't wait until Lance got home to tell him about their appointment. Ms. Sarah watched Lily while they went to the house viewing. Lance and Elizabeth pulled up in the driveway and Elizabeth just sat there. She knew in her gut this was it, this was their home. They got out and looked around and everything was wonderful, they both agreed

Chapter 41

they loved it. The price of the house was a few thousands over what they actually were approved for. Elizabeth explained to the sellers their situation and the seller advised Lance and Elizabeth to call their lender and see if they would increase the loan. When Lance and Elizabeth got home and talked it over and went over their options. The next day Elizabeth called the loan officers only to hear they were not able to do an increase. When Elizabeth got off the phone, she was devasted and full of disappointment, Lance comforted her and put Lily down for her nap before he left for work. Elizabeth laid down as well. She had a hard time sleeping and she begin to pray to God for help and asking God when will they ever get a breakthrough. Elizabeth finally took a short nap, after praying. That short nap was just what she needed to recharge. Elizabeth decided to call the seller and update them on the outcome. Elizabeth told the sellers the truth and what happened next took her by complete surprise. The seller said, "for some reason they could not stop thinking about us and they decided to drop the price on the amount of their loan. Elizabeth became silent and overwhelmed with joy. The Lord had heard her prayers and she was grateful. Elizabeth could not wait to share the amazing news with Lance. She called him right away, Lance was confused, because he knew they could not afford the asking price. Elizabeth filled him in and explain everything, it was really

The Long Road Ahead

happening and they would soon be first time home buyers. It was like a dream to Elizabeth, a loving husband, house of their own, two wonderful children and Elizabeth was soon to graduate. Elizabeth wasted no time packing. It would be a couple of months before they closed on the house. Packing made it real for her, they didn't have much and Elizabeth didn't want to bring her past into her present. Elizabeth wanted A fresh start with new beginnings, but she was still carrying the weight of her past that would soon take its toll on her and her family.

Chapter 42

Lance and Elizabeth didn't have much to move, so the transition to the new house was easy. Lance's twin brother Larry helped them move. It was the happiest day of their life and one of their greatest accomplishment together. Together with a few clothes, a Tv, 2 beds, a crib and a few wedding gifts they were home. Every time Elizabeth would leave to go out, on her way back home, she would begin to cry from feeling overwhelmed with joy and happiness. Elizabeth and Lance started going to church regularly, she didn't have to worry about seeing Aaron, because he had moved away and only came occasionally. Elizabeth and Lance were still learning the concepts of marriage and the hidden vows that seems to manifest when all is going so well. Communication was not a strong suit for Lance and Elizabeth and they had trouble agreeing on most things. Lance and Elizabeth realize that there was a lot of things they didn't not know and disliked about each other. They loved

The Long Road Ahead

one another that was one thing for sure, but they really didn't know one another. They fought verbally it seemed like all the time and the next day was like it never happen. Elizabeth was still broken from her past and every now and then it would spill over into her happily ever after. Lance out of the blue, he brought up the subject of Elizabeth getting her tubes tied. Elizabeth could believe the words that came out of Lances, mouth. Getting her tubes tied was something Elizabeth never wanted to do and he knew that. To Elizabeth tying her tubes was like getting an abortion. She could not believe or even comprehend why he was asking her to violate her body. After that everything started shatter. The voices came back and the pain of past failures surfaced. Elizabeth's world began to shift and she mentally felt abandoned, lost and alone. Elizabeth had wanted more children and she hated him for even bringing that awful suggestion to her. Why didn't he just get a vasectomy? Why did he ask her to suffer such a procedure? Who was this man standing in front of her? It was all too much to think about and Elizabeth happy medium took a turn for the worst. Words between Lance and Elizabeth became few and it seemed they argued more than talked. Elizabeth began to despise Lance and did everything without him. Elizabeth worked out her frustration on her own and loneliness begin take hold. Elizabeth felt lost in the world they created for themselves.

Chapter 43

Aaron surfaced again and started calling and trying to be friends with Elizabeth. Elizabeth and Lance became strangers in their marriage. Elizabeth just wanted to feel alive, and talking with Aaron was a good start, she thought. It felt good, it was the thrill of someone caring and paying attention to her, that gave her the satisfaction she carved. Elizabeth knew it was wrong, but she wanted the attention, even if it was bad attention. Lance and Elizabeth grew farther apart as she, gave him what her asked for and they awaited the day she dreaded, "the tuba ligation". The day of the procedure Elizabeth had a lot of anxiety and Lance knew it and never said a word. They drove to the hospital in silence and when they arrived Elizabeth was prepped for the procedure. The surgical teamed rolled Elizabeth back to the OR. They stopped where Lance was waiting and the doctor asked Elizabeth was, she sure about having this procedure done. Elizabeth looked over at Lance and

The Long Road Ahead

begin to cry, she was yelling from inside NO please don't do this, but nothing came out and before she knew it, she was in the recovery room. She felt like her world no longer existed and her control was taken away once again and mentally Elizabeth's life had no meaning. Lance and Elizabeth drove home in silence.

It was like the day of her an abortion, only worst. From that day forward Elizabeth was never the same.

Chapter 44

Elizabeth had finally graduated college and started a new career. She worked hard but could never keep a job. Depression had the reigns in her life. A dark cloud had followed Elizabeth ever since that day. She had been in and out of mental institutions, but nothing could break the heaviness which had over took her. Elizabeth had been seen by psychiatrist after psychiatrist and tried every medication on the market. Elizabeth was diagnosed was as manic bipolar with mixed schizophrenia. Elizabeth couldn't function in her the world, agitation, frustration, angry, hurt, shame and bitterness filled her heart. Elizabeth was in a pit and dint care if she lived or died. Elizabeth dint agree with the diagnoses of her therapist, but heavily medicated is how she made it through the day. Elizabeth didn't want to feel the emptiness inside of her. Lance never recognized the pain she was in. He lived if everything was normal, never talking about what happen. Lance and Elizabeth

The Long Road Ahead

were fighting constantly. Some days were good, but the bad days outweighed the good. Elizabeth was vengeful she spent her days, wanted Lance to feel her pain and misery. Elizabeth couldn't see anything passed her pain. Not her children, her self-worth, nor Lance love for her and the thought of moving forward seems impossible.

She became self-centered and in a fog of her own. Elizabeth went to church every day and got a bandage for her wounds, that always seemed to come right off, as soon as she left out the building. Most Sunday Elizabeth and Lance went over his parents' house for Sunday dinner. Lances' parents decided to order out and Elizabeth went with Mrs. Vanessa to pick up dinner. Elizabeth became good at wearing masks to cover up what was really happening inside and out. They were talking and Mrs. Vanessa got on the subject of the tuba ligation. Elizabeth was surprised that she even knew about it. What happen next left a big gaping hole right in the middle of Elizabeth chest. Mrs. Vanessa said "am so glad you two decided to listen to me about getting a tubal, y'all don't need no more children." Elizabeth couldn't believe the words that had come out of her mouth. She was the cause or the mastermind behind all this chaos. Elizabeth 's heart pounded faster and faster. She wanted to jump out the car. Her mind raced, how could he? Coward. She thought as rage took over her. How

Chapter 44

could he let them into their circle? Elizabeth hated Lance even more, she hated what was happening between them and their marriage. The anger inside Elizabeth had taken over, fire filled her eyes and at that moment Elizabeth had an out of body experience. She felt her body no longer belonged to her. Elizabeth was lost and alone and didn't care any longer.

Chapter 45

Lance and Elizabeth arguments became emotionally, verbally, and physically abusive. It was the only way to ease the pain, anger and raged from the inside her. Noah and Lily were scared for their mother and tried everything in their power to make her feel better. Nothing seemed to work. Lance was clueless and lost but never said a word. He didn't even realize what he had done. He didn't understand her rage, which made Elizabeth outburst even worst. Sundays were the only good days, but that only lasted for half the day. Aaron reached out to Elizabeth again. They begin to talk on the phone more at night especially when Lance was sleeping or at work. Talking to Aaron was Elizabeth comfort from all the mixed emotions. He made her laugh and feel like she was important. Elizabeth needed that, her self-worth with Lance was nonexistent. They talked about having an affair, but never had the time to commit the act. He wanted to and she just wanted a quick fix to ease her pain.

Chapter 45

Mentally Elizabeth just wanted to feel love and fill the emptiness that she felt inside. Aaron and Elizabeth phone affair went on and off for months almost a year. Lance never suspected a thing. Elizabeth took it as he never really cared what she did. They were hanging on by a tread, Elizabeth wanted to leave. But Elizabeth still loved him and she still wanted him. She meant to love him, but she ended up hurting him instead. It was hard to see past all the hurt and damaged that had been done. Aaron and Elizabeth continued their phone affair, but it wasn't fun any more for her. Elizabeth needed more as the emptiness grew. The sneaking around and lying was eating her up inside, she had to come clean.

Chapter 46

Elizabeth wanted tom make things better between her and Lance. They were marriage and had two wonderful children. Elizabeth finally decided to get what her and Aaron had done off her conscience. She sat down with Lance and told him everything. Lances' response shocked her; he was not a man of many words and showing his emotions was not one of his strengths. He practically just brushed it off. Deep inside he knew something was going on, but he loved her. It was enough for Elizabeth. Saying you love someone and showing you love some were not the same. The action from him only added more fuel to Elizabeth's fire. She wanted him to be anger at her, to yell at her. She needed it more than ever at that moment. She needed him to be upset and hurt. She needed that, to know that he loved her. They went their separated ways and never spoke of it again, as always. Elizabeth wanted things to be better, but the communication between them was broken. Aaron

Chapter 46

seemed to reach back out to Elizabeth, it was like he knew things were not so good. They would talk constantly then nothing for a while. Elizabeth begin to reach out to him and it went on and on. Until Aaron got married and Elizabeth felt like a fool in many ways. She felt used and ashamed. Why did she allow herself to believe his lies and deception? Elizabeth knew what kind of person he was and what his motives were, but she still tried make the fantasy world a reality. Unable to take any more damage to her heart. Elizabeth was overwhelmed by her pain, shame and mixed emotions and at that moment Elizabeth contemplated suicide as her only option. Elizabeth had allowed her emotions to control her destiny. The voices in her head were stronger than ever and she just wanted to rest, to get away from it all, until she could make sense of it all. Elizabeth took some pills to ease the pain and the voices sweetly told her "To take a little more it won't hurt, it will only help." Elizabeth slowly began to slip deeper and deeper into what she thought was a peaceful rest. Her eyes begin flood with tears of fear and regret of her actions. All Elizabeth could see was Noah and Lily laughing, smiling and then everything went dark.

Chapter 47

Elizabeth woke up in Lance's arms with him yelling," Please Elizabeth wake up, what did you do? I love you; I need you Please". The smell of vomit was overwhelming and the cries from Lily were amplified. Elizabeth was confused and baffled at what she had done. What was she thinking? She just wanted to rest, not leave this earth. Elizabeth cried and begged Lance not to call the ambulance, she assured him she was okay. Elizabeth explained to Lance that she had thought about suicide, but would never do it. Elizabeth just wanted to rest and make the voices stop; she didn't realize what she was actually doing. Lance helped Elizabeth to the bathroom and took good care. He helped her by getting her cleaned up and in bed. Lance was worried about Elizabeth and kept a close eye on her all night. Lance didn't know what to do, he didn't realize things were this bad. The night past and Elizabeth slept like a baby. The next morning Elizabeth had to faced her reality and she just didn't

Chapter 47

want to get out of bed. She didn't want to face the reality of what happen and the people she hurt by her actions. Elizabeth just knew Lance had enough and he was going to leave her. Lance didn't want go to work that day and Lily didn't want go to school. Elizabeth got up and assured them both that she loved them and she would be fine. Elizabeth knew she had to keep moving forward no matter how much the pain inside demanded to be felt. She had Noah and Lily to think about. Lance was trying, but why was it not enough? He was no match for the battles raging inside of Elizabeth. Elizabeth had got a new job working for the state. She worked hard to kept herself busy and distracted from her pain that constantly tried to stay at the surface. Lance and Elizabeth were still very distant and were not communicating well. They had some good days but as always it seemed the bad days over ruled the good. It was to the point where they were just living a mechanical life. They were intimate but only out of obligation.   Elizabeth had abruptly stopped seeing her therapist and she continued to work hard in her new career, all while masking the balled up unhappy feeling from within. Elizabeth met a charming guy friend at work. His name was Shawn. He was cute, quite friendly, funny and gave Elizabeth the attention she longed for. He appeared to be just what Elizabeth needed at the time, a good friend. Their friendship started to flourish and Elizabeth was distracted in having the time

The Long Road Ahead

of her life. They were emailing one another every day, going on lunch dates and texting continuously. He knew she was married, but that didn't stop him from trying to pursue her. He knew she was not happy and he played on every ounce of her unhappiness. Lance was clueless and couldn't care less and Elizabeth was having the time of her life. Lance was lost in playing house and playing his games.

Elizabeth started visited Shawn at his home. She would leave in the early afternoon and be back hours later. Lance never questioned her whereabouts. Aaron reached out to Elizabeth again and they started off right back where they left off. It was like nothing ever happened, she let him in once again. Aaron always seemed to make his way back into her life and she always let he back in. Elizabeth was thrilled by all the excitement going on in her life, it masked the pain she tried so hard not to feel. Going to work was the highlight of Elizabeth life, she felt wanted, needed, important, liberated and appreciated. The attention gave her a natural high and kept her energized.

Chapter 48

Elizabeth was seeing Shawn more and more. At first, it was fun and exciting the thrill of it all was unreal.

They would just talk and watch movies and that's all Elizabeth wanted some excitement, fun, attention and friendly affection. The thrill of being with Shawn and then talking with Aaron in the late hours was like a game to her and she enjoyed playing it. The game kept Elizabeth's mind occupied and her heart bandaged. It was like they knew her, what she wanted, what she desired and made her feel wanted. The more Lance ignored her, the more she more she got involved in search of the feeling of validation. Everything was going fine, until Elizabeth realized Shawn wanted more, just like Aaron. Aaron was far away, so it was easy to make excuses and play with fire without getting burned, but Shawn was close and in reach. Elizabeth now felt trapped and somehow obligated.

The Long Road Ahead

Elizabeth wanted to somehow get out and break it off with Shawn, but she was trapped in a hard decision of how could she now get out of the dark web she created. Why couldn't she just stop? Why was it so hard to just turn it off? Elizabeth was addicted, but she never intended for their friendship to get to this point. They worked together and she couldn't just run away and quit her job just yet. There was too much at stake, Elizabeth feared the outcome if she continued entertain this relationship. Elizabeth had no one to talk to, this was not a road she intended to turn down. Elizabeth decided to turn to with Lance. She didn't outwardly tell him, still playing games in her mind. Instead, she made up a scenario, as if she had already committed the act with Shawn. Elizabeth couldn't tell her reality from the world she created. She informed Lance how sorry she was, she tears formed up, because it felt so real and she begin to plead to him for his forgiveness. Lance faced Elizabeth and looked at her with a clueless expression and said "it's okay". He didn't show any feeling or even seemed moved by her action. His next words were; "I love you and am sorry I was not the man you needed me to be". Those very words cut Elizabeth like a two-edged sword. Lance wiped her tears and continued to say "were okay just don't do it again please". Elizabeth was devasted and felt a sense of rejection, that was not the response she expected. Elizabeth was confused and didn't know what she was looking for

Chapter 48

from him, but feeling sorry for himself was not it. She just wanted Lance to feel to her pain, her hurt and to see the dark pit that had her held captive. She couldn't see past her brokenness, that he really did love her and he just didn't know how to express it the way she needed it. The lack of emotions and expressions of Lances love for Elizabeth only pushed her to pursue Shawn. Shawn was falling in love with Elizabeth, but she didn't feel the same. Elizabeth just wanted to feel wanted by her one true love "Lance". She was just in love with the fact that someone saw her and marled at her existence and before she knew it, they were in Shawn's bedroom and Elizabeth had allowed Shawn to invaded their vows. Elizabeth forgot her vows, her worth and who she was, all because Elizabeth allowed her past to dictate her future. It happened so fast, it was dark and then it was over. Elizabeth close and opened her eyes praying she would wake up and this was all a bad dream. But it was real it did happen and Elizabeth got ready to leave, but Shawn wanted her to stay. "Why are you leaving" he asked her? Elizabeth frantically replied "am so sorry, you don't understand; I belong to him; I never meant to hurt him, I was angry, this was a terrible mistake, am so sorry, this is not who I am". Confused Shawn, as he watched Elizabeth run out the door in disbelief of their encounter. Elizabeth was devastated by what she had allowed to happen and left with her head hanging low in

The Long Road Ahead

despair. Driving home she begin shaking from anxiety and fear of the unknown begin to overtake her and she pulled and over on the side of the road and screamed at the top of her lungs.

The words of unfaithfulness and adulterer tormented her mind as she looked up in the mirror and didn't recognize the monster that stared back at her from inside. Elizabeth felt worthless, ashamed, lost, unloved, defeated and broken. She was extremely disappointed in her actions and who she had become. Elizabeth wanted die from the pain and betrayal she caused that had entrapped her very existence. How could she face Lance after, he had forgiven her and she did it anyway? They had their problems, but this was different. Elizabeth had destroyed their marriage vows, their family, her character, everything she believed in. She never wanted it to get to this point, but playing with fire cause her to suffer the effects of the fiery darts from enemy that was inside of her. Elizabeth went home to face Lance; she chose to turn down that road and now she had to face the consequences. He was playing one of his games and never questioned her whereabouts. Elizabeth's life was shattered into a million little pieces. It seemed hopeless to think that this tragic event with everything else on top of it could be fixed. She took a long shower and laid down with hopes of never waking up. Elizabeth

Chapter 48

couldn't sleep, the pain was too much to bear, she wanted so bad for Lance to come in and hold her.

She wanted to tell him, she betrayed him. She wanted him to yell at her, tell her he hated her and end it all. Lance came to bed after finishing up his game. He kissed her good night and went to sleep. Elizabeth was furious, she felt like she was exploding, screams from within tormented her and the room begin to spin and she needed to release. Her brokenness turned quickly into bitterness. Why couldn't he feel her pain? Why couldn't he hold her and make it all go away? Aaron text that night and Elizabeth replied back, they talked all night and Aaron made her forget her pain for a moment. It was getting late and Elizabeth finally ended the call, but not before she confessed to Aaron about the day, she lost their baby. Aaron was shocked and then become quite furious with Elizabeth for keeping that from him and from that night forward they said good bye and she didn't hear from him for a while.

Chapter 49

Noah and Lily were getting older. The arguing between Elizabeth and Lance only got worse, but they never separated. They fought, they made up, it was a viscous congoing cycle. After an intense blow up between them, Noah decided to move in with his dad who now lived out of state. During that time Lance lost his job, for lying on his application and Elizabeth world was changing fast and she couldn't take it any longer. She got in her car and drove and drove until she ended up at Tracey's house, one of her dear friends she met in college. Tracey opened the door and Elizabeth fell into her arms and cried historically. They talked and talked, Elizabeth told her everything and prayed, they cried and they laughed. Tracey was a good friend, as it got later in the day, she said "my friend it's time you go home now to your husband; God is faithful, just trust Him". Elizabeth and Tracey said their goodbyes and Elizabeth headed back home fearful of the unknown. The word of her friend made a lot of

Chapter 49

sense at that moment. Elizabeth and Lance talked; well Elizabeth did most of the talking. Lance never shared his feelings or emotions, he just listened, he was good at that. But his silence really pushed Elizabeth's buttons hard. How could she reach him, if he didn't share what was going on inside? No matter how much she yelled and screamed Lance never had any words to say. He just sat there with a blink look as always. Elizabeth just wanted to be free from the black hole she lived in daily, but nothing was helping. The hole kept getting deeper and deeper and the only glimpse of hope she had was faint. Elizabeth ended up quitting her job with the state, she couldn't bare showing up after what happen between her and Shawn. Elizabeth was at her wits end and nothing she tried in her own strength seemed work. Every time a peak of a broke through, something bad would happen. Elizabeth and Lance got in a major fight which involved the police and Lance ended up going to the hospital. The cops asked Lily a few questions and she was terrified and Elizabeth was angry at them for questioning her. That night no charges were pressed, but the officers insisted one of them had to leave that night. Elizabeth and Lance were separated for the first time in years. Elizabeth was shattered/ broken, as she tucked Lily into bed and apologized to her for being angry. Elizabeth couldn't go on like this. She was at the bottom with no way out and at that moment she fell to her knees and cried out to the

The Long Road Ahead

Lord;" I surrender all the my hurt, pain, my shame, my rejection, my abuse and disappointment". The Lord met Elizabeth right there that night, in all her pain and filled the emptiness she couldn't fill herself. Elizabeth had been searching for love that cost her everything, when the love she needed cost her nothing and was there all the time. Elizabeth longed for Lance and Lance longed for Elizabeth. Elizabeth couldn't see that she had all she needed right in front her, until it wasn't there anymore.

The next day Elizabeth called Lance and he came over so they could talk. They talked and for the first time in a long time Elizabeth realized, she still loved him and didn't want to have a world without him.

Elizabeth struggled with the feeling that entrapped her mind, but she was determine to stay with Lance and make it work. Elizabeth dove deeper to her walk with the Lord trying to find answers and make sense of everything. She wanted deliverance from the all the turmoil that lay inside of her. She wanted to let down the walls she had built, but it was hard. Letting down her walls meant being vulnerable and susceptible to being hurt again. The more she tried the harder it got, but giving up was not an option this time around. Elizabeth found her inner strength and she had made up in her mind that, she no longer wanted to live in this place of

Chapter 49

bondage. The more Elizabeth pressed forward and tried to forgive, the more the pain wanted to burst to the surface and demand its place. Elizabeth knew she had to keep pressing for herself, her marriage and her children. She didn't want to see Noah and Lily suffer any longer. Noah would visit every now and then on the weekends and holidays. Elizabeth heart was breaking to only see him from time to time, this was not the life she pictured for them. Lily blamed her mother for Noah leaving and Lily blamed Noah for leaving her behind in all the chaos. Lily and Noah had a close relationship and she cried often, because she missed him dearly. The pain that entrapped Elizabeth in a deep dark hole, had also destroyed her family. It had been years, but the memory of her past constantly chased away her confidence to overcome. Elizabeth had a hard time believing that she deserved better and became content of what was. Elizabeth friend Grace was having her own problems and their relationship was broken. Elizabeth was alone. God was her only source of help and Elizabeth hung tightly to that. Most days Elizabeth found it hard to trust anyone, even God at times. The days ahead seemed different but the same. Lance and Elizabeth were trying their best to reconcile their marriage. They seemed to agree on one thing and one thing only. He was deeply in loved her and she was madly in

The Long Road Ahead

love with him. She was the last piece to his life's puzzle and he was the perfect verse to her favorite love song.

Chapter 50

Elizabeth got invited to an afternoon church service by a church friend. She was tired and didn't want to go, but decided to go anyway. That evening at church everything that could go wrong went wrong, even the church service. It didn't seem to bother Elizabeth and she begin to worship the Lord, like it was just her and God it the room. A lady of the church came over and begin to prophecy everything that was happening in Elizabeth's life. Elizabeth sobbed in surprise of her knowing. She prayed for Elizabeth and the anointing rushed over Elizabeth like a raging sea! The lady whisper into Elizabeth ear softly, but with authority "Daughter its Over! Elizabeth yelled and it felt like weights of baggage fell off of her and she felt at peace. Elizabeth left that evening full of joy unaware of what had just taken place. What it really meant. All she knew is she felt wonderful, lighter and free spirited. Elizabeth couldn't wait to get home and share her experience with Lance.

The Long Road Ahead

Later that evening when she arrived home, she happily told Lance and Lily about the service and all she experienced. He was really happy for her, she seemed different. Lily hugged her mother. They watched a movie with Lily and afterwards went to bed. That night Lance held Elizabeth and apologized to her for not being the man she needed and he held her tightly. Elizabeth felt his love for her for the first time in a long while. That night they knew one another again as for the first time in a long while, though an intimate and passionate encounter. It was a magical night, just like in the beginning. Elizabeth fell deeply back in love with Lance as she cried tears of joy and drifted off to sleep in his arms. Elizabeth woke up with joy in her heart and a new outlook on life. She couldn't explain the feeling she had, but she loved it and never wanted to be without it again. Everything was going great a few days passed and Elizabeth was the happiest she had been in a while. Lance had a new job and they were on this new journey of being a family again. There was an unexplainable peace, that filled their hearts and home. Elizabeth smiled; she knew that only God could give that kind of peace. Elizabeth started to realize that, the church service she went to, she not only received her joy back, but deliverance took place as well. Elizabeth felt free and her mind was clearer. There was no loud voices and the dark holes, the walls, depression, emptiness, bitterness, shame, raging

Chapter 50

anger and hurt of the her past haunted her no more. Elizabeth's found hope in the darkest place hour of despair. The chains that kept Elizabeth a prisoner in her past, had broken off and her eyes were opened. Lance and Elizabeth decided to trust God for their relationship and family. They were better together. So, they made the choice to continue to press forward in the journey set before them as husband and wife. They realized that they needed to work on their communicate and daily they learned to stop fighting each other and start fighting the problem together.

THE End of the Beginning

Printed in the USA
CPSIA information can be obtained
at www.ICGtesting.com
LVHW050201130124
768898LV00003B/18